THE

Basic·Basics·

HOW TO
🍴 COOK 🍴
FROM A–Z

JANET MACDONALD

GRUB STREET • LONDON

Published by Grub Street, The Basement, 10 Chivalry Road
London SW11 1HT

Copyright © 1998 Grub Street, London
Text copyright © 1998 Janet Macdonald
Jacket design Adam Denchfield Design
Book design Graeme Andrew
Design copyright © 1998 Grub Street
Illustrations: Andrea Darlow

Reprinted 2002

British Library of Cataloguing in Publication Data

Macdonald, Janet
Basic basics: how to cook from A-Z
Cookery
I. Title
641.5

ISBN 1 898697 98 1

Printed and bound in Great Britain by Biddles Ltd
www.biddles.co.uk

Whilst every effort has been made by the author and publishers to ensure that the
information contained in this book is accurate neither can accept responsibility for
any errors contained herein.

CONTENTS

FOREWORD

Although I have been cooking for over 30 years, I still have to look up some basic recipes. (This is despite, or possibly because of, the fact that I have also been writing cookery books for nearly 10 years. When you spend most of your time in the kitchen creating and testing new dishes it is hardly surprising that the proportions of eggs to milk for a simple custard disappear from your memory.) Many of my friends who are also experienced cooks tell me they suffer the same problem, so this book is partly for them and partly for all those new cooks who need guidance on what to buy and how to cook it.

As well as the specific details of buying, storing, preparing and cooking various ingredients, information on basic cooking techniques and my suggestions on essential kitchen equipment are all presented in an easy-to-find A-to-Z format. I also have a few tips for new cooks:

- Never mix metric and imperial measurements given in a recipe – they are not exact conversions.
- With the exception of cakes, where exact measuring is essential for success, quantities given in recipes (both in this book and in others) are only guidelines. At the end of the day, the texture and taste of any given dish is a matter of personal taste.
- Always try new dishes out on your family before you cook them for guests, then you can be sure they will turn out right.
- Always ask guests if they have any food allergies before you decide on the menu.
- Make friends with your suppliers – the butcher, fishmonger and greengrocer. Tell them what you want and what you intend to do with it, and ask their advice on how to cook things, such as certain cuts of meat. Never be afraid to ask – even if the butcher doesn't cook, you'll find plenty of people in the queue who will gladly tell you.
- If you are cooking on a tight budget, buy your food in street markets or farm markets, where everything will be much cheaper than in supermarkets.
- The best piece of advice I can give any cook is stay in the kitchen and keep an eye on things while they are cooking. Once dishes are in the oven, or simmering on top of the cooker, you can leave the kitchen – provided that you set a timer to call you back before something goes wrong.

I hope this book will help you turn into the sort of cook who enjoys their time in the kitchen.

COOKERY BASICS

ACIDULATED WATER

Some fruits and vegetables (such as apples or celeriac) discolour when they are cut. To prevent this, they should be dropped immediately into 'acidulated' water - cold water which has some lemon juice or vinegar added to it. To each litre (2 pts) of water, add 2 tablespoons lemon juice or vinegar.

BAKING BLIND

This is the process of precooking the pastry-case for a flan or open pie. After rolling out the pastry and placing it in the tin, lay a piece of greaseproof paper on top of the pastry and fill the dish with dried beans or peas (keep a jarful for this purpose) or special ceramic 'beans', before baking for the time stated in the recipe.

BARBECUE

Cooking food out of doors, over hot 'coals' of charcoal, or ceramic bricks when the barbecue is heated by gas or electricity. The general effect is the same as grilling, but you can add smokey flavours to the food by adding special wood chips or herbs to the coals. If you barbecue frequently, it is worth buying wire containers to hold meat or fish.

BARDING (sometimes called larding)

Adding a layer of fat to dry cuts of meat to prevent their drying out during cooking. This is often done with beef sirloin or veal roasting joints, and you can either ask the butcher to do it for you, or lay some slices of streaky bacon over the meat yourself. An alternative method of barding is to make little slits in the meat and push slivers of fat into them.

BASTE

Pouring fat or marinade over meat while it is roasting, to coat the surface with flavours.

BLANCHING

The process of subjecting fruit or vegetables to a short burst in boiling water, then cooling them rapidly by plunging into very cold water. The purpose is to loosen skins for easy removal (as with tomatoes or peaches) or to set the colour and flavour (often done before freezing). Where instructions specify a time for blanching, start timing when the items go into the boiling water. Do not confuse this process with the gardener's process of blanching vegetables such as asparagus or endive by covering them to exclude light.

BOIL

Liquids are boiling when the surface is constantly agitated by the heat rising from below. Most foods do not need to be cooked at a constant boil (one exception is pasta) and the heat can be turned down to simmer when boiling point has been achieved.

BRAISE

Cooking meat in the oven in an open roasting tin, starting with a small amount of liquid in the tin. This liquid evaporates during cooking, creating steam which tenderises the meat in the process.

CASSEROLE

Cooking meat slowly in the oven in a closed pot, with vegetables and plenty of liquid – the original 'one-pot' meal. Traditionally, this is a method of cooking cheaper cuts of meat, as the long slow cooking process tenderises it.

CHOP

Using a knife to cut food into uniformly sized pieces with a series of quick movements. A knife with a triangular shaped blade is best for chopping. Place the food to be chopped on a chopping board, hold the tip of the knife on the board with the fingers of one hand, and use the other hand to move the knife up and down as you chop the food.

'Rough' chopping means large uneven pieces, 'fine' chopping means very small pieces. With large vegetables, it is best to halve the item to give a flat surface on the board, then slice most of the way through it in two directions before chopping in the third direction.

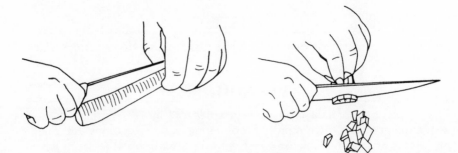

CREAMING BUTTER AND SUGAR

The process of mixing, then beating, butter and sugar together until it resembles a smooth cream, used in the early stages of cake-making.

DE-GORGE

Some vegetables, such as cucumber, have excess water which you get rid of in the process of de-gorging. Slice the vegetable and lay the slices in a colander, sprinkling salt generously over each layer. Leave them for 30 minutes, during which time the salt will have drawn the moisture out. Rinse well, then dry before cooking.

DICE

The process of cutting food into small cubes. See chopping.

EXTRACTING JUICE

Citrus fruits can be halved and squeezed, either by pressing them onto a squeezer, or by pressing a fork into them and squeezing with your hand. Other fruits or vegetables should be chopped very finely, or processed with a liquidiser before straining.

FLATTENING MEAT FOR ESCALOPES

This is done partly to tenderise the meat (especially steak which may not be top quality) and also to make the meat thinner so that it will cook quickly and thus not dry out (important with delicate dry meats such as veal). To avoid splashes, put the meat between greaseproof paper or in a plastic bag, then whack it all over with the base of a heavy saucepan, or meat mallet.

FRYING

There are three types of frying: deep frying, where you immerse the whole of the item in hot fat; shallow-frying, where you cook items one side at a time in a thin layer of fat; and stir-frying, where the items are cut small and fried very quickly in a minimal amount of fat, being constantly stirred and turned while they cook. You can stir-fry in a frying-pan, but a round-bottomed wok is easier. It is important when deep-frying to fry only a few items at a time, as too many items will reduce the temperature of the oil and the food will end up soggy and fat-logged.

GREASE

The process of preparing tins or dishes so that the contents do not stick. You can use oil or butter/margarine, either applied thinly with a pastry brush, or smeared on from the inside of the wrapper. Then put a little flour in and shake it to coat the layer of grease.

GRILL

The process of cooking items close to the heat-source, either the gas flame or a red-hot electrical element (or barbecue). Lining the grill pan with foil before cooking will make it easier to clean. Do not salt meat before grilling, as this can make it tough.

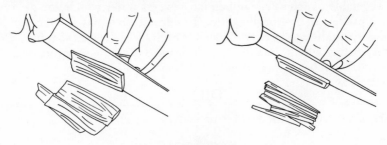

JULIENNE

Cutting ingredients into match-stick sized pieces. Proceed as for chopping, but cut long pieces instead of small cubes.

KNEAD

Kneading incorporates yeast into flour and other ingredients, to give a smooth texture to bread and pastry. To knead, turn the dough out onto a floured surface. Flour your hands and use one to knead while the other turns the dough. Reach over the dough and use your fingertips to bring the outside into the middle, then press it down with your knuckles. Give the dough a quarter turn and repeat.

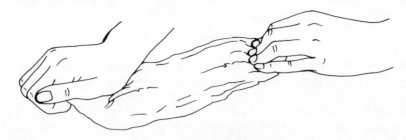

LIQUIDIZE

Reducing food to a pourable consistency with the aid of a liquidizer or food processor, usually for soups or sauces.

LUKE-WARM

This is a term used to describe liquid at medium heat. Sometimes described as 'hand-hot', it means liquid in which you would be happy to hold your hand.

MARINATE

The liquid in which you marinate food is called a marinade. The liquids are mixtures of oils, lemon juice, vinegar or wine, spices or herbs, or yoghurt. The purpose is to tenderise the food and add flavour to it. As the acid ingredients may cause an effect on metal containers, marinating should be done in a glass or ceramic container, or in a sealed plastic bag, which you then turn over at intervals to spread the marinade over the ingredients. Any marinade which is left over can be used as a sauce for the cooked food, but should always first be brought to the boil to kill any bacteria which it may have picked up from the raw food.

'OVERNIGHT'

Many recipes tell you to leave ingredients or mixtures 'overnight'. This just means 'for at least 8 hours' – there is nothing magical about night-time, and 8 or more hours during the day will do just as well.

POACH

Cooking foods such as fruit, eggs or fish in liquid which is gently simmering.

POT ROAST

Cooking meat or poultry slowly on top of the cooker in a closed pot with a small amount of liquid. This is a good technique for cheaper cuts of meat. Vegetables and herbs may be included.

PURÉE

Fruit or vegetables reduced to a thick liquid consistency, either by pressing them through a fine sieve, or by using a food processor or liquidiser.

ROAST

Cooking meat or vegetables in the oven in an open dish, usually with a little fat which may be used to baste the food during cooking.

ROUX

A mixture of melted butter and plain flour, used to thicken sauces, soups and stews. To make a roux, melt the butter in a pan and gradually stir in the flour, then cook for a couple of minutes stirring constantly. The roux can then be transferred to a small bowl or jar until needed, when it should be stirred into the liquid to be thickened. To use it straight away, stir the other liquid into the roux, a little at a time. There are three kinds of mix, white, fawn and brown; the colour depends on the cooking time.

RUBBING-IN

The process of mixing fat into flour before liquid is added to make a dough. Put the flour into a mixing bowl. Cut the fat, which should be at room temperature, into eight or ten pieces, add it to the bowl, then use a knife or pastry blender to cut the fat into very small pieces. Put both hands into the mixture and rub a little amount between the thumb and the first two or three fingers of each hand until the mixture resembles breadcrumbs. It is easiest if the thumbs move towards the first finger.

SAUTÉ

Frying food quickly in a small amount of fat – much like stir-frying.

SEALING MEAT

The process of frying the meat before braising or casseroling it, to seal in the juices. Sometimes known as 'browning'. The fat should be hot, and only a few pieces of meat should be sealed at a time, otherwise the fat will cool and the meat will not seal properly.

SIFT

Some recipes require that flour should be sifted. This lightens the mixture by loosening the grains of flour and thus incorporating air. (There is no need to automatically sift all flour, as modern production methods produce better textured flours than used to be available.) You can buy special flour sifters, but an ordinary round-bottomed sieve will do. Hold the sieve over the mixing bowl with one hand and pour the flour into it, then tap the sieve lightly with the other hand so the flour drops into the bowl.

SIMMER

Cooking in liquid which is barely boiling. To simmer, watch the surface of the liquid until it starts to boil, then turn the heat down so that the liquid is barely moving.

SLICE

Cutting ingredients into even-sized flatpieces. For most ingredients, place them on a cutting board so that the knife cuts through them down onto the board. For items which are too large, use a fork to hold the item steady and cut so that the knife goes towards the fork rather than towards you.

SLOW COOKING

Also known as Crock pot cooking, this is a method of cooking with very low heat for several hours, now used to mean 'in a purpose-made slow cooker' (stews and casseroles are slow-cooked). An excellent way to tenderise cheaper cuts of meat, and to ensure that a tasty meal is ready when you return from work. The ingredients are heated to boiling point before putting them in the slow cooker, which then simmers very gently.

STEAM

Cooking ingredients in the vapour from boiling liquid. An excellent way of cooking vegetables without losing flavour and vitamins through boiling.

STERILISE

To prevent moulds and bacteria invading your home-made jams or chutneys, the jars should be washed thoroughly then sterilised. This is done by placing the clean jars in a moderate oven (180°C/350°F/ Gas Mark 4) for 5 minutes.

STEW

Cooking meat or poultry slowly on top of the stove, with vegetables and plenty of liquid. Traditionally, this is a method of cooking cheaper cuts of meat, as the long slow cooking process tenderises it. Many people believe that a stew tastes better if allowed to cool overnight, then reheated. Dumplings can be cooked in the liquid just before serving.

STONE, CORE, SEGMENT AND SKIN FRUIT

Fruits with stones have a 'seam' down one side. Cut down this seam and on round the fruit, deep enough to feel the stone with the knife. Take one side of the fruit in each hand, and twist in opposite directions to separate. Some stones cling to the flesh and have to be cut out. (See separate entry for mangoes).

Apples and pears have a pipped core. To bake an apple, the core has to be removed while leaving the apple whole, so a semi-circular corer must be used. Otherwise, cut the fruit in quarters from top to bottom, then cut diagonally to remove the core and pips. The quarters can then be cut into smaller segments.

Stone fruit often has a loose skin which can be pulled off gently with the help of a knife. Otherwise, and with cored fruit, the skin should be peeled thinly with a sharp paring knife or peeler.

SWEAT

Encouraging ingredients to release their juices at the beginning of cooking, by putting them in a closed saucepan with a little fat.

TOAST

Cooking bread or other yeasty baked foods close to a heat-source, either the gas flame or red-hot electrical element of a grill, or in a purpose-made toaster. A good way of making a tasty dish from slightly stale items.

TOP AND TAIL

To remove the stalk or stem and flower remains or roots of fruit such as gooseberries or vegetables such as radishes.

WHIP/WHISK

Beating cream, egg-white or cake-mixtures until it becomes more or less solid. Stages of whipping are known as 'soft peaks' (when it can be pulled up to a peak which will gradually fall over) or stiff peaks (when the peaks remain in place).

ZEST

 The outer surface of citrus fruit peel, which contains aromatic oils and juice. You'll need a special zesting 'knife' to remove it from the whole fruit before peeling by pull zester towards you.

A NOTE ON OVEN TEMPERATURE CONVERSIONS			
CELSIUS	**FAHRENHEIT**	**GAS**	**DESCRIPTION**
110°C	225°F	¼	Cool
120°C	250°F	½	Cool
140°C	275°F	1	Very low
150°C	300°F	2	Very low
160°C	325°F	3	Low
170°C	325°F	3	Moderate
180°C	350°F	4	Moderate
190°C	375°F	5	Moderately hot
200°C	400°F	6	Hot
220°C	425°F	7	Hot
230°C	450°F	8	Very hot

BASIC EQUIPMENT –
THE ESSENTIALS

When you are new to cooking, the displays of cooking equipment in the shops can be bewildering. There is so much to choose from, and it all comes in different shapes and sizes so you don't know what to buy, or how you're going to afford it all. The good news is that you don't actually need that much, and you don't necessarily need the expensive versions. As well as listing the items you do need, I've added some tips on what sort to buy.

With most items, it is wise to buy the best you can afford, as this lasts longer and thus costs less in the long run.

COOKER

The choice is between electric and gas cookers. (Ranges such as Agas require slightly different cooking techniques, and are outside the scope of this book.) Professional cooks like gas for its instant response to altered heat settings, but this is not essential for novice cooks.

If possible, choose a cooker with an eye-level grill. You can make toast on this grill (if you are prepared to stand and watch it) and thus will not need a separate toaster. The oven should have at least two shelves.

For the financially or spatially impoverished, 'baby' cookers are available and are good value.

Microwave ovens are useful, either as an addition to the ordinary oven, or as a sole method of cooking in a small kitchen. However, the techniques required to use them to their best advantage are rather different, and thus outside the scope of this book. (See *Basic Basics Combination and Microwave Handbook*, also published by Grub Street.

APRON

The purpose of wearing an apron is to protect your clothes from splashes and smears, so it should be big enough to do this, with a bib part that comes up close to your chin. Wipeable material saves on washes, and a pocket is useful.

BAKING TRAYS

As well as using them for actual baking, you can use a baking tray to place various other items (such as pies) on before putting them in the oven.

BOTTLE OPENER

If buying a separate bottle opener, choose a sturdy one with a handle that is easy to hold.

BOWLS

You need a selection of bowls in various sizes – one large one for mixing pastry, cakes, etc., at least one medium sized one for beating eggs, cream etc., and some smaller ones for holding small quantities of ingredients, breaking eggs, storing left-overs, etc. Unbreakable glass, plastic or stainless steel are better than enamel, which chips if dropped.

BULB BASTER

Plastic basters are safer than glass. The bulbs perish quite quickly, so it is best to buy cheap basters and replace them frequently.

CAKE TINS

If you want to make cakes in fancy shapes, you can usually hire special tins from kitchen equipment shops. Otherwise, simple round cake tins are the best, and best of all are the 'springform' type which spring open when you undo the clip. This makes it much easier to remove the cake. Shallow cake tins can also be used to make quiches.

CAN OPENERS

Cheap metal can-openers work just as well as the various more expensive fancy types. Most incorporate a bottle opener.

CASSEROLES (WITH LIDS)

You need two – a big one for casseroles, pot roasts and other bulky dishes, and a smaller one for baked puddings such as rice. Pyrex or stoneware are best value, cast iron will last for ever but are heavy.

CHOPPING BOARD

Can be wooden or the new hygienic plastic materials. If you can afford it, buy several to avoid using the same one for foods which should be kept separate, such as cooked and raw meat.

CLING FILM

Useful for wrapping sandwiches and covering food before refrigerating it. Buy the 'microwave safe' sort if you have a microwave.

CLOTHS

Plain cotton tea-clothes can be bought in batches very cheaply and are useful for drying dishes, wiping up spills and, when folded sufficiently, as insulation when lifting hot dishes. For hygiene, they should be washed frequently, which is why you need several.

COLANDER

Metal is better than plastic, as it can then be used as a makeshift steamer. A single long handle is more useful than two small handles.

CORKSCREW

These come in various types. The simplest version, which is just as effective as any, is called 'the waiter's friend' - it folds flat for storage and incorporates a small penknife for removing metal foil.

DEEP-FAT FRYER

You can deep-fat fry in a saucepan full of oil with a straining basket, but this is the cause of so many domestic fires that you would be advised to buy a purpose-made electric deep-fat fryer.

ELECTRIC LIQUIDIZER

Excellent for making soups, purées, and fruit drinks. Most come complete with a separate coffee (or spice) grinder. If you have a food processor or a hand blender, you won't need a liquidizer.

ELECTRIC MIXER

Not essential, but a blessing if you make a lot of cakes or do a lot of whisking and find it irksome to your wrist muscles.

FOIL

Kitchen foil is invaluable, for wrapping cooked food before it goes in the fridge, or for covering food in the oven. Remember that the shiny side reflects heat, and will slow down the cooking process.

FOOD PROCESSOR

Invaluable for liquidizing, making purées, or shredding, slicing and grating large quantities of food. The only thing they don't do is whisk, as their action is slicing, not beating. Although the electric versions are quite expensive to buy, the better makes will last for many years. (Mine is still going strong after 27 years).

FRYING PANS

Buy either top-quality cast-iron or non-stick frying pans, or cheap non-stick ones which you keep for a year then replace. If you like omelettes, keep a separate small omelette pan.

FUNNELS

Not essential but very useful. A large funnel allows you to decant liquids without spilling, a small funnel allows you to refill salt and pepper shakers easily.

GARLIC PRESS

Not essential – use the flat blade of a large knife to crush the garlic instead.

GRATER

Buy the four-sided sort which stands on its own and has different sized grating surfaces. This will allow you to grate vegetables, cheese, and nutmegs.

GREASEPROOF PAPER

Useful for placing over the surface of sauces to prevent a skin forming, and for lining cake tins.

HAND-HELD ELECTRIC BLENDER

Comparatively inexpensive, these are invaluable for making soups or sauces. You just put the business end of the blender in the pan and whizz away, without having to use another pan, or a sieve to remove lumps. Buy one which comes with a set of mixer heads as well.

JELLY BAG

You can use pieces of butter muslin to strain various ingredients (such as yoghurt when making cream cheese) but a jelly bag is easier to use (and very cheap to buy). It is simply a fine mesh bag with four loop handles which can be hung up to drip.

KETTLE

Buy either a kettle which whistles when it boils, or one which switches itself off when it has boiled. Cordless electric kettles are more expensive, but more convenient (and safer). If you live in a hard-water area, choose a kettle with a built-in filter.

KITCHEN PAPER

Invaluable for wiping fingers, wiping up spills, and de-greasing fried food.

KNIVES

A good sharp knife is essential for all cutting tasks. You will need one medium sized knife to cut meat, chop vegetables and herbs, and at least one small knife to peel vegetables and fruit. Serrated blades are less useful than straight blades. You will also need a sharpener for your knives.

LEMON/ORANGE SQUEEZER

You can squeeze citrus fruit in your hand, but it is less messy to use a squeezer. The best and cheapest are the simple dishes with a conical centre to press the fruit onto, and a pouring lip for transferring the juice. You can get them with their own reservoir underneath, or to fit over a jug. Choose one with holes which let the juice through while retaining the pips on top.

MILK SAVER

This is a small glass disk which you put in the saucepan when heating milk, which prevents the milk boiling over.

MEASURING CUPS

American cooks use the cup to measure dry or wet ingredients, but a 'cup' is a specific measurement, not just any old cup you happen to have handy. If you want to cook from American recipe books, or from recipes found on the Internet, it is worth investing in a set of cup measures (¼, ⅓, ½ and whole cup)

MEASURING JUG

This can be either plastic or unbreakable glass, and should have measurements marked on it.

MEASURING SPOONS

Stout plastic is better than flimsy metal for these spoons. They come in sets of half-teaspoon, teaspoon, dessertspoon and tablespoon. You cannot be sure that other spoons are the correct size.

MIXER OR WHISKS

If you have a strong wrist, all you need is one or more balloon whisks. Otherwise, hand-operated mixers are useful, mixing machines with a separate bowl are good but cost more. In between are small battery-operated mixer/liquidisers.

OVEN GLOVES

Not essential if you have plenty of cloths, but gloves do protect the back of your hands from the edges of the oven.

PASTRY BRUSH

Buy two – one for sealing and glazing pastry, the other for greasing tins (and applying warmed butter to bread for sandwiches). Ordinary house-painters brushes work just as well as purpose-made pastry brushes and may be cheaper.

PASTRY CUTTERS

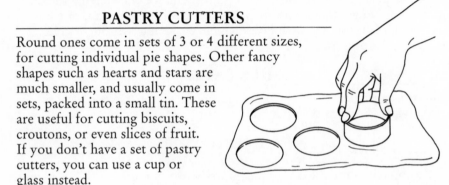

Round ones come in sets of 3 or 4 different sizes, for cutting individual pie shapes. Other fancy shapes such as hearts and stars are much smaller, and usually come in sets, packed into a small tin. These are useful for cutting biscuits, croutons, or even slices of fruit. If you don't have a set of pastry cutters, you can use a cup or glass instead.

PEPPER MILL

Essential for grinding fresh black pepper. The classical type is cheapest and usually works better than modern fancy types.

PESTLE AND MORTAR

Used for crushing and grinding small amounts of dry spices, or crushing fresh herbs. A useful implement, but not essential, as putting the items in a plastic bag and crushing them with a rolling pin or other heavy implement works just as well.

POTATO BAKERS

A device with a handle and 4 metal spikes, onto which you push the potatoes. The spikes conduct heat into the centre of the potatoes, speeding up cooking time. Useful, but an ordinary metal skewer works just as well.

POTATO MASHER

You can mash potatoes with a large fork, but a purpose-made masher is quicker and easier.

RAMEKINS

Small round dishes with flat sides, these are like little soufflé dishes. They usually come in sets of six, and are useful for serving little baked custards or coddled eggs, or for pre-dinner nibbles such as nuts or olives.

ROASTING TINS

You can buy cheap turkey-sized roasting tins around Christmas time. Otherwise buy good quality non-stick tins, or large ceramic dishes, ideally with a pouring-lip.

ROLLING PIN

Used for rolling pastry, rolling pins can be made of wood or sometimes glass. If you don't have a rolling pin, use a wine bottle instead.

SALAD SPINNER

These come in two types – a simple wire basket which you close and swing round by hand (preferably outdoors!), or the enclosed plastic type which has a handle which you turn to rotate the inner basket, creating a centrifuge effect which spins the water off the leaves inside. If you don't have room for either of these, rinse the salad leaves, shake most of the wet off, then place them in a clean tea towel, gather up the corners and swing the towel by hand.

SAUCEPANS

There are many pretty enamelled sets of saucepans available, but in general they are expensive and not that good quality. Enamel chips when dropped, so is not a good idea. Non-stick pans are useful (especially for milk) but good stainless steel pans are practically non-stick anyway. Aluminium saucepans are very cheap, but are not a good idea as aluminium is thought to be one of the contributory causes of Alzheimer's disease.

Saucepans, and their lids, should have handles which do not transmit heat, unless you are prepared to use a cloth every time you handle them.

SCALES

The more people you will be cooking for, the larger your scales need to be. For two people, scales which measure up to 1 kilo (2 lbs) should be sufficient. The measuring bowl should be detachable for washing.

SCISSORS

Sharp scissors are necessary to cut open packets, remove bacon rinds, snip herbs, and various other kitchen tasks. They should be washable.

SIEVES

You probably need two sieves – a large one for soups and a medium one for flour, fruit and sauces. A tea-strainer will serve for smaller tasks such as sieving ground spices.

SKEWERS

Short skewers are useful for holding meat or poultry in shape. Longer skewers are used for kebabs or other barbecued foods – these should be flat-bladed so the food does not slip round when you turn it over.

SPATULA

There are two sorts of spatula – the long thin-bladed type, for spreading icing or jam on cakes, and the shorter broad sort for scraping bowls. The latter is more useful, and will also spread icing and jam.

SPOONS

You need a selection of cooking spoons in various sizes. For stirring whilst cooking, especially with non-stick pans, wooden spoons are best. Buy cheap ones and replace them regularly. Perforated or slotted spoons are useful for removing items from hot liquids.

STEAMERS

You can buy electric steamers (which often incorporate a rice cooker), but cheaper, and producing a quicker result, are steamers which fit on top of saucepans. Stainless steel is excellent, but Chinese bamboo steamers are cheaper, work just as well, and you can stack several of these on one saucepan, thus cooking different items on one ring.

STOCKPOT

Nothing more than a very large lidded saucepan, a stockpot is invaluable if you want to make your own stock, but also useful for cooking pasta. Buy one big enough to hold at least 7 litres (12 pints) of water.

STRAINERS

You will need at least one strainer for various tasks such as straining stocks or fruit. Ideally, you should have two, one round based and one conical based. Both should fit at least one of your saucepans and bowls. You can get cheap ones made of plastic with plastic mesh, which are good enough, but stainless steel is better. Non-stainless metal is not a good idea, as they will rust.

STRING

Thin kitchen string can be used for many purposes, from trussing poultry to tying a bunch of herbs.

TIMERS

Simple clock-type timers are invaluable if you aren't staying in the kitchen while a cake or time-crucial dish is cooking

TOASTER

Not necessary if you have an eye-level grill and are prepared to watch the proceedings. Otherwise, choose a toaster which has wide cooking slots, and ideally one which has sandwich toasting attachments.

VEGETABLE PEELER

Not necessary if you have sharp knives and a steady hand, but otherwise useful for rapid removal of thin amounts of skin. Choose the type which you prefer.

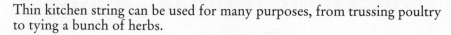

THE BASIC STORE CUPBOARD

With a set of basic items in your store cupboard, you can always produce a tasty meal, or repair a disaster when you're entertaining. You can make your own additions to these lists, but start with:

- Almonds, flaked. Toast these in the oven and keep them in an air-tight jar to sprinkle on puddings, ice-cream, curry rice.
- Anchovies, tinned or bottled, preferably in olive oil which can be kept to flavour other dishes after the anchovies have been used.
- Baking powder and bicarbonate of soda.
- Beans, dried and tinned – red beans for chilli con carne, butter beans to add to vegetable stews, flageolet beans for soups.
- Boudoir biscuits or trifle sponges.
- Butter.
- Frozen chicken livers.
- Tinned chickpeas, to purée for hummus, add to soups, or vegetable stews.
- Cocoa powder.
- Cornflour.
- Curry powder or paste.
- Eggs.
- Vacuum-sealed flan bases and glaze, to produce an instant pudding with a tin of fruit.
- Flour – plain and self-raising, plus strong flour for bread-making. Either of these can be wholemeal if you prefer.
- Bottles of chopped garlic, ginger, pesto.
- Tubes of garlic purée.
- Dried herbs –thyme, oregano, rosemary, but not basil or parsley which have little flavour when dried.
- Honey.
- Jellies.
- Ketchup.
- Dried lentils –small red ones for soups, dark green 'Le Puy'ones for French country dishes, big yellow ones for dhal.
- Tinned mandarin oranges for a flan or to perk up a jelly.

- Tinned mangos or mango purée for quick puddings.
- Sweet mango chutney.
- Real maple syrup.
- Good mayonnaise.
- 'Breakfast' milk.
- Dried wild mushrooms.
- Tinned mushy peas.
- Dijon and grain mustard as well as English mustard powder.
- Dried noodles for quick snacks or stir-fries.
- Oils for cooking and salad dressings – sunflower, olive, walnut or hazelnut, sesame.
- Herb oils for salad dressings – tarragon, basil, garlic.
- Olives, green or black, according to your taste.
- Grated Parmesan cheese – not as good as chunks of the real thing, but a useful stand-by.
- Dried pasta in a variety of shapes, including some tiny ones to add to soups.
- Frozen puff and shortcrust pastry.
- Pepper, black and white.
- Easy-pour frozen prawns for quick prawn cocktails.
- Redcurrant jelly, marmalade, apricot jam and strawberry jam, all good for perking up puddings, topping ice-cream or adding to gravy.
- Rice.
- Salt.
- Soy sauce.
- Spices – chilli, cinnamon, cumin, coriander.
- Stock or Oxo cubes.
- Sugar – granulated and caster, plus icing sugar for cake-icing.
- Tinned tomatoes (whole or chopped), to add to spaghetti sauces, soups etc.
- Tubes of tomato purée.
- Tomato sauce.
- Pourable treacle.
- Tinned tuna.
- Wine and cider vinegar.
- Wonton and spring roll wrappers to turn leftovers into tasty snacks.
- Worcester sauce.
- Dried yeast.
- Natural yoghurt in small pots. These keep well if unopened.

FOOD AND COOKING SAFETY TIPS

Germs and other unpleasant health-threatening organisms thrive and increase rapidly in the warm humid atmosphere of a kitchen. The essential rule of kitchen hygiene is to keep everything clean – wash surfaces, pots and pans thoroughly as soon as they have been used, change all your wiping and drying cloths at least once a day, and do not let fragments of food lie around in corners. Always wash your hands before handling food and keep separate bowls for preparing food and washing up.

Check 'sell-by' and 'use-by' dates before buying food and only buy what you can use before those dates expire. When buying any sort of food which comes in a sealed container made of plastic, reject any where the container has swollen or 'blown'. This is caused by bacterial action and is a sign that the contents will be unsafe to eat.

Food should be refrigerated as soon as possible after purchase. Any stored food that starts to grow mould, or smells or tastes 'off' should be thrown away.

Meat, poultry and egg dishes should be treated with particular care, due to the risk of salmonella and other organisms. Cooked meats and raw meat should be kept separate, and ideally you should not use the same knives or chopping boards for raw and cooked meats. Always wash your hands thoroughly after handling any of these foods, before handling other foods.

Potatoes develop poisonous substances if exposed to light long enough to turn the skin green, so they must be kept in the dark. Dried beans and peas may contain toxins, so they should be boiled for 10 minutes at the start of cooking, then the water should be changed.

All cooked foods should be allowed to cool to room temperature before being put into the fridge. Frozen meat should be thawed completely before cooking.

Some shell-fish such as mussels can contain toxins unless they are alive when purchased (unless already cooked or frozen). Cook them on the day of purchase. Any that have open shells before cooking, or that stay closed when cooked, are dead and should be thrown away.

Due to the risk of salmonella from raw eggs, and of listeria from cheeses made from unpasteurised milk, foods containing these should not be given to pregnant women, very young children and very old people.

Some people also suffer life-threatening allergies from various foods, including nuts, food colourings, or gluten (found in wheat flour), so it is wise to ask guests if they suffer from allergies before you prepare food for them.

Alarming though all this may sound, in fact simple common sense is all you need to prepare healthy food.

You also need to apply common sense to avoid injuring yourself when cooking. Sharp knives are less likely to slip and cut you than blunt knives, and saucepans are less likely to spill hot contents on you if you keep the handles turned away from the front of the cooker. Steam can scald as badly as boiling liquid, so keep your face and hands away from pans as you lift lids.

Wipe up spills from the floor immediately so you don't slip on them, and wear low heeled shoes in the kitchen, especially when carrying hot dishes. Tie back long hair so it won't trail across hot burners when you bend down near the cooker, and avoid loose clothing (especially sleeves) that could do the same. Hot splashes are a constant danger in the kitchen, so wear long sleeves to protect your arms and a large apron which will protect your skin as well as your clothes.

A-Z OF BASIC FOODS

APPLES

TO BUY

Apples should feel firm, and have no bruises, holes or splits. They should smell fresh. Reject any which smell musty or feel flabby. To eat raw choose an 'eating' variety such as Gala, Golden Delicious, or Cox. To cook for pies, purées, sauces or baked apple, choose a 'cooking' variety such as Bramley or Reverend Wilkes. For open-topped tarts where you want to arrange slices of apple, choose a crisp eating apple such as Golden Delicious, McIntosh, or Granny Smith.

TO CLEAN

Wipe each fruit over with a damp cloth, then dry before storing.

TO STORE

For long-term storage, of several months, lay the apples out on a tray so that they are not touching, then store in a cool dark place. For medium-term storage, of a few weeks, apples can be kept in a plastic bag in the fridge. Over the short-term, say a few days, they can be kept in a fruit bowl on the side-board. Apple cooked in the form of purée or sauce can be frozen for up to 12 months.

TO PREPARE AND COOK

For baked apples, remove the core and make several slits in the sides to allow the steam to escape during baking. Fill the core space with brown sugar and, if you like, raisins or powdered cinnamon. Place the apples in a dish with a little water in, and bake at 180°C/350°F/ Gas Mark 4 for 35 - 40 minutes. The best apples for baking are Bramleys.

For open topped tarts, cut the apple into quarters from top to bottom, and cut out the core. Do not peel, but slice each section thinly, dropping each piece into acidulated water (see page 5) to prevent it discolouring. To retain the shape of the slices, add sugar at the beginning of the cooking time and avoid stirring. Use only enough water to cover the bottom of the pan and cook gently in a lidded saucepan, checking every couple of minutes that the pan is not dry. The apples should make their own liquid as they cook.

For purées, apple sauce, or pie fillings, proceed as above but peel each section before slicing.

APPLE SAUCE/PURÉE

4 tablespoons water
a squeeze of lemon juice

1 kg (2 lbs) cooking apples
 (ideally Bramleys),
 peeled and sliced
25 g (1 oz) sugar

Put the water and lemon juice in a large saucepan and drop each piece of apple into it as you peel and slice them, stirring occasionally to ensure each piece is coated with juice. (This is to prevent the apple discolouring.) When all the apple is done, add the sugar, cover the pan and stew the apple gently for 10 - 15 minutes. Stir at intervals until the apple has broken down into a fluffy mass. Serve straight away, or freeze for later use.

APPLE PIE

juice of 1 lemon
a little butter to grease the
 pie-dish
1 kg (2 lbs) cooking apples
 (ideally Bramleys),
 peeled and sliced

225 g (8 oz) caster sugar
6 cloves (optional)
1 recipe shortcrust pastry
 (see page 111) or 2 sheets
 ready-rolled shortcrust pastry
a little milk for glazing

Put the lemon juice into a bowl half-filled with cold water. Preheat the oven to 220°C/425°F/ Gas Mark 7. Grease the pie-dish lightly with the butter. Peel, core and slice the apples, dropping each piece into the lemon water. When all the apples are ready, drain them briefly and put them in a saucepan with all but 1 tablespoon of the sugar. Put a lid on the pan and cook over medium heat for 6 - 8 minutes, until the apples begin to lose shape. Meanwhile, divide the pastry in half, roll each piece to form a circle a little larger than the dish, and lay one piece in the dish, leaving it untrimmed.

When the apple is ready, lift it from the pan with a slotted spoon and spread it on top of the pastry. Place the cloves equally round the dish and push them into the apple. With a pastry-brush, brush a little milk round the pastry on the edge of the dish, then lay the other piece of pastry on top. Press the edges together, trim off the spare pastry and either use your fingers to flute the edge, or use the tip of a knife to make a pattern. Make a small hole in the middle of the pie to let steam escape. If you want to use the spare pastry to make a decoration of leaf-shapes, do so, sticking these down with a little more milk. Finally, paint the whole of the top with milk before putting the pie in the oven to cook for 25 - 30 minutes, or until the top is golden brown. Take it out of the oven and sprinkle the rest of the caster sugar over the top while it is still hot, then serve it hot or cold.

APRICOTS

TO BUY

Apricots come in three forms – processed, dried, or fresh. Fresh apricots are mostly imported from the Mediterranean in early summer, but can be disappointingly mealy and tasteless. If all you intend to do with them is make jam, it hardly seems worth the expense when there are many excellent apricot jams or conserves available. For most recipes, dried apricots are easier to handle and more flavoursome. The best, and consequently most expensive, dried apricots are the tiny Hunza fruits. You may only find them in health food shops or Indian grocers.

TO STORE

Eat fresh apricots within 2 days of purchase. Dried apricots can be kept for many months in an airtight container.

TO PREPARE

Rinse fresh apricots under a cold tap before eating or cooking. Short of using a very sharp knife on it, the skin is difficult to remove, but since it is not tough, there is no need to do so. To remove the stone, cut the fruit all round its circumference, then twist the two halves in opposite directions.

Dried apricots, unless marked 'ready to eat' should be soaked for 30 minutes in boiling water. When using them to stuff meat, chop them before soaking as they are easier to handle then.

TO COOK

Fresh or dried apricots can be stewed with a little added sugar, or converted to jam with more sugar.

APRICOT FOOL

150 g (6 oz) dried apricots,
   soaked in hot water
2 - 3 tablespoons caster sugar
a squeeze of lemon juice
300 ml (10 fl oz) whipping cream
25 g (1 oz) flaked almonds, toasted

Drain the apricots and save the water. Reduce them to a purée in a liquidiser, adding a little of the cooking water if necessary, taste and add sugar and lemon juice as you feel necessary. Whip the cream to the soft peaks stage, then fold in the apricot purée. Transfer the fool to serving dishes and sprinkle the toasted almonds on top.

ASPARAGUS

TO BUY

Fresh green asparagus can be bought all year round from large supermarkets, but is best (and least expensive) in early summer when the English crop is harvested. It normally comes bound into bundles, but sometimes the thin sticks known as sprue are sold loose. Fresh asparagus should feel firm, and it should snap if bent. Reject flabby or soft sticks. Imported white asparagus is sometimes available, either fresh or bottled. You can also buy tinned asparagus.

TO CLEAN

Fresh asparagus needs no more than rinsing under running water.

TO STORE

Store asparagus in the fridge for up to 48 hours. If you have room, stand it upright in a jar of water after cutting a thin slice from the bottom of the stems. It can be frozen for up to 12 months.

TO PREPARE

White asparagus should have the stalks peeled. Green asparagus should not need this. Instead, hold each stalk near the bottom in one hand, and bend the stick until it breaks. The top should be tender enough without peeling.

TO COOK

After preparation, retie the bundles and cook them standing upright, tips on top. Cook them in boiling water deep enough to cover the stems, but leave the tender tips to steam above the water. Use new potatoes to hold the asparagus upright, and cover the tips and top of the pan with foil. (If you do not have a deep saucepan, you can cook asparagus in a coffee pot.) They should take 5 - 6 minutes to cook. Alternatively, lay the stems in a steamer and steam them for 5 - 6 minutes. Drain them well and serve hot with melted butter or Hollandaise sauce (see page 139) for a simple starter, or cut them into short lengths and mix with cooked pasta.

Asparagus can also be grilled or roasted in the oven. Brush a little melted butter on the spears, then give them 5 - 7 minutes under a hot grill, or 10 minutes in the oven at 190°C/ 375°F/ Gas Mark 5.

AUBERGINES

TO BUY

The 'standard' aubergine is long and deep purple, but oriental grocers may have small violet or white ones, or even bunches of tiny green ones. Handle aubergines with care, as the stalks can be prickly. They should feel firm and have shiny skin. Reject those which are dull and flabby.

TO STORE

Store aubergines in a cool place, but preferably not the fridge, which can make them flabby. They can be frozen for up to 9 months, but should be blanched first.

TO PREPARE

Standard wisdom is that aubergines need to be degorged to get rid of bitterness or excess moisture, and also to prevent them absorbing too much fat. None of this is true, and degorging has the disadvantage of discolouring the flesh, so don't bother. Just trim off the remains of the stem, wipe the skin with a damp cloth, and cut the fruit as needed for your recipe. There is no need to remove the skin.

TO COOK

To fry aubergines, cut them into slices or cubes, then cook these in a few teaspoons of very hot oil. As they cook, their natural juices will moisten them.

To grill, paint the top surface with a little oil, grill until that side is cooked, (6 - 7 minutes), turn and repeat.

To roast, cut the aubergine in half lengthwise, score the cut surface into diamonds, paint with a little oil and roast at 220°C/425°F/ Gas Mark 7 for 25 - 30 minutes. You can then scoop out the flesh and stuff the skin with a mixture of cooked rice, nuts, raisins, herbs and cheese before baking for a further 10 - 15 minutes.

AUBERGINE 'CAVIARE' TO SPREAD ON BREAD

1 large aubergine	2 - 3 cloves garlic, finely chopped
2 tablespoons olive oil for cooking, plus 1 more tablespoon	1 tomato, peeled, deseeded and finely chopped
2 - 3 shallots, finely chopped	salt and black pepper
	juice of 1 lemon

Prick the aubergine several times, then bake it at 180°C/350°F/ Gas Mark 4 for 30 - 40 minutes, until it is tender right through. Take it out of the oven and let it cool, then cut it in half and scoop out the flesh. Meanwhile, heat the oil in a frying pan and fry the shallot and garlic until translucent. Drain and mix in with the aubergine. Mix in the tomato, season, taste and add lemon juice to your taste. Finally stir in some fresh olive oil before serving.

AVOCADOS

TO BUY

Avocados are ready to eat when they give a little as you gently squeeze them. They should not feel soft (overripe) or absolutely hard, and should not have any discoloured patches on the skin. Although they do not look as attractive as the smooth bright green ones, the Haas avocados with knobbly almost black skin have the best flavour.

TO STORE

Store not-quite-ripe avocados at room temperature for 2 - 3 days, when they will ripen. They can be kept in a bowl with fruit. To speed up the ripening process, put them in a paper bag in a warm place such as the airing cupboard. Once ripe, store them in the salad crisper in the fridge. Avocados can be frozen as pulp for up to 2 months. Add 1 tablespoon of lemon juice per avocado to prevent discolouration.

TO PREPARE

Avocados discolour when cut, so have some lemon juice handy to dip or paint on cut surfaces. Cut lengthways all the way round the avocado as far as the stone. Twist the two halves in opposite directions to separate them. Stick a fork or skewer into the base of the stone and ease it out gently. Use the whole avocado, as they will turn black within a couple of hours if you try to keep them.

To serve slices of avocado, cut the slices before peeling. Avocado halves can be served with the cavity filled with vinaigrette, mayonnaise, or prawns and prawn cocktail sauce.

GUACAMOLE

This is a creamy dip of avocado, served with tacos or other crisp biscuits, either as part of a Mexican meal or on its own.

2 shallots	2 large avocados, peeled
1 - 3 cloves garlic	and mashed
1 fresh green chilli, deseeded	2 tablespoons chopped parsley
and roughly chopped	salt and pepper
1 large tomato, skinned,	juice of 1 lemon
(see page 151), deseeded	2 teaspoons of sugar (optional)
and roughly chopped	

Put the shallots, garlic, and chilli in a liquidizer and whizz them for about 20 seconds, add the tomato, avocados and parsley and whizz again until everything is smooth. Add salt, pepper, lemon juice and sugar to your taste, whizz again briefly to incorporate these, then turn the guacamole out into a bowl. Alternatively, mash the flesh with a fork and chop the other ingredients finely before stirring them in. Cover with cling film if not serving straight away.

BACON, GAMMON AND HAM

Bacon comes from the back and sides of the pig, gammon from the front end, and ham from the back legs.

TO BUY

Bacon rashers for frying come smoked or unsmoked (sometimes called 'green'), as 'back' with an eye of meat or as streaky, with streaks of alternate fat and meat. 'Dry cure' bacon is probably the best buy, as it doesn't give off a watery white juice during cooking which other types can. Which you buy is a matter of taste. If prepacked, they also come with or without rinds - there is no particular advantage in having the rinds left on, and since all you do is cut them off and throw them away, they are a waste of money.

For boiling, buy bacon or gammon joints, or ham. Hams can also be baked. Ham hocks are a cheap way to buy ham, and these can be boiled or baked.

For cooked ham, see page 54.

TO STORE

Uncooked vacuum-packed gammon or ham can be stored in the fridge for up to 4 weeks, as can pre-packed bacon rashers. Once opened, the contents of these packages, or other bacon, ham or gammon, should be used within 5 days. Take what you don't use out of its original wrapping and rewrap it in cling film or a sealed plastic bag. Bacon can be frozen for up to 8 weeks.

Cooked joints or hams can be kept in the fridge for up to 4 days.

TO PREPARE

Some bacon, gammon or ham joints can be very salty, and should be soaked in at least two changes of cold water for several hours before cooking. Leg joints may have a plastic cover over the bone – remove this before cooking.

TO COOK

Start boiling joints in cold water. Bring this to the boil, then remove any scum and turn the heat down so that the water is barely simmering.

Cooking joints too fast makes them tough. Joints up to 4.5 kg (10 lbs) should be cooked for a basic 20 minutes, plus a further 40 minutes for each kilo. Larger joints for 15 minutes plus a further 30 minutes per kilo.

Joints can also be baked, for the same times as above, in an oven preheated to 180°C/350°F/ Gas Mark 4. To retain the moisture, wrap the joint in foil before cooking.

Bacon rashers and gammon 'steaks' can be fried or grilled. Either remove the rind, or snip through this every 2 cm (1") to prevent them curling up during cooking.

BANANAS

TO BUY

There are many types of bananas, including their relations the plantains which are used in Indian and Caribbean cooking, but the bananas found most easily are the yellow sweet ones. In general, it is best to buy them while they are barely yellow, or even still green, and let them ripen to the stage you like at home. They are very easily bruised, and the riper they are, the more damage bruising does to them, making them quickly rot. However, if you want very ripe bananas for making cakes or banana bread you can often buy them much cheaper. The more black there is on the skin, the riper and softer the inside will be. Banana 'chips' (slices of banana dried and fried until they are hard) are a good and tasty snack food.

TO STORE

Bananas should be kept at room temperature and not in the fridge. If mashed to a pulp with lemon juice and sugar, they can be frozen for up to 6 months.

At room temperature, how long they will take to deteriorate beyond the usable stage depends on how ripe they were when bought, and how warm your house is, but it is wise to check them every day. If bought still green, in the average house they should keep for 5 - 7 days. Banana chips should be kept in an air-tight jar, where they will keep for several weeks.

TO PREPARE

For most purposes, all you have to do with a banana is peel it and slice it. However, do not do this until the last minute, as they start to blacken as soon as they are exposed to the air. Alternatively, drop the slices into acidulated water straight away.

TO COOK

Bananas can be barbecued or grilled, in which case leave the skin on until they are cooked. They can also be battered and fried to make banana fritters, baked with orange juice in the oven for 30 minutes at 190°C/375°F/ Gas Mark 5, or mashed and added to cakes. Banana 'bread' is actually a loaf shaped cake, which can be eaten as it is or spread with butter.

BANANA BREAD

50 g (2 oz) softened butter	2 large bananas, sliced and mashed
50 g (2 oz) caster sugar	175 ml (6 fl oz) natural yoghurt
2 eggs, beaten	50 g (2 oz) chopped nuts (optional)
225 g (8 oz) self-raising flour	

Grease and flour a 900 g (2 lb) loaf tin and preheat the oven to 180°C/350°F Gas Mark 4. Cream the butter and sugar together until you have a soft light mixture. Beat the flour, eggs, bananas and yoghurt into the mixture with the chopped nuts. Mix in well, then spoon the mixture into the tin and level the top. Bake for 55 - 60 minutes, or until it feels firm when gently pressed. Leave to cool in the tin for 10 minutes before turning out onto a wire rack to cool completely.

BATTER

For pancakes, Yorkshire pudding or Toad in the Hole, use this batter made with plain flour and milk.

125 g (4 oz) plain flour	300 ml (10 fl oz) milk
2 eggs	(full cream or skimmed)

Put the flour into a mixing bowl, break the eggs into the centre and mix them into the flour, adding the milk a little at a time. Using a whisk will help prevent lumps. Leave the batter to stand at least 30 minutes.

To make sweet pancakes, add 1 tablespoon caster sugar to the mixture before adding the milk.

To coat fish or vegetables for frying, use this batter made with self-raising flour and water.

125 g (4 oz) self raising flour	150 ml (5 fl oz) water
pinch salt	

Put the flour and salt into a mixing bowl, then gradually whisk in the water, continuing until the batter is smooth and lumpless. (You can use beer or lager instead of the water.)

TO STORE

Batter can be stored in the fridge for up to 48 hours, but should be whisked again before use, adding a little water to thin it if necessary.

YORKSHIRE PUDDING

Make batter from the first recipe above, but use half milk and half water instead of all milk. You can use a clean roasting tin, or the tin in which you have roasted the meat. You'll need about 25 g (1 oz) lard, or 2 tablespoons vegetable oil or dripping, and the fat, tin, and oven must be very hot. (Oven temperature 220°C/425°F/ Gas Mark 7) Give the batter a last-minute whisk, take the roasting tin from the oven and pour in the batter. Put the tin back in the oven immediately and cook for 35 - 45 minutes, until the pudding is well risen and golden brown all over. To make individual puddings, put ½ teaspoon fat in each compartment of a deep bun tin, put this in the oven until the fat is very hot, divide the batter between the compartments and cook for 15 - 20 minutes.

TOAD IN THE HOLE

This is just a Yorkshire pudding with sausages or chops in it. Make up Yorkshire pudding batter as above. Cook the sausages or chops (or a mixture of both) in a deep roasting tin as usual. Thirty minutes before the end of their cooking time, take the tin out of the oven, pour out all but 2 tablespoons of the fat, pour in the batter and return the tin to the oven for 30 - 40 minutes.

BEANS – DRIED

TO BUY

Different types and sizes of beans take different times to cook, so although you can buy packs of mixed beans, it is best to buy them separately.

TO CLEAN

You should not need to clean beans, but it is wise to check that packets of smaller beans do not include small stones.

TO STORE

Store, in the packet, in a dry cupboard. Once the packet is open, keep the unused beans in a sealed box or jar. Dried beans keep a long time but start to deteriorate after 6 months and will then take longer to cook. Leftover cooked beans can be kept in the fridge in a plastic bag or sealed dish for 24 hours.

TO COOK

All dried beans should be soaked overnight, then boiled for 10 minutes in fresh water, drained, and simmered in more fresh water. Salt prevents beans softening, so don't add salt to the cooking water until the beans are almost done. Beans are cooked when they are tender right through, and they should then be drained.

Cook:
- mung or aduki beans for 20 - 30 minutes
- haricot beans for 50 - 60 minutes
- red kidney or black beans for 60 - 90 minutes
- butter beans for 60 - 75 minutes
- borlotti or pinto beans for 75 - 105 minutes

HOME-MADE BAKED BEANS

450 g (1 lb) dried beans - haricot, borlotti or butter beans
3 - 4 teaspoons mustard powder
3 tablespoons tomato paste
600 ml (1 pt) boiling water
225 g (8 oz) soft brown sugar

3 - 4 medium onions, peeled and quartered
225g (8 oz) streaky bacon (optional)
pepper
salt

Precook the beans in plain water (no salt) until they are just tender. Drain them and throw away the water. Preheat the oven to 120°C/ 250°F/ Gas Mark ½. Put the mustard powder and tomato paste in the empty bean saucepan and mix it to a thin paste with a little of the boiling water. Add the sugar and the rest of the water and stir until the sugar has dissolved. Put the onions, the bacon and the drained beans into a large casserole, sprinkle the pepper over them, then pour in the liquid. Cover the casserole and bake it for 4 hours, taking it out of the oven every hour to give it a stir and make sure there is plenty of water. After 4 hours, remove the lid, add salt and continue cooking for another hour, stirring half way through to push the top layer of beans down. It should end up with a layer of browned beans on top.

BEANS – GREEN

TO BUY
Fresh green beans should snap if bent in half – reject any which feel flabby. You can buy frozen green beans, but they have very little taste and a poor texture, so there is little point. Frozen broad beans, on the other hand, can be quite good.

TO STORE
Fresh beans should be used as soon as possible after purchasing. If you are not using them straight away, store them in the salad drawer of the fridge.

TO PREPARE

Broad beans – wear rubber gloves, as the inside of the pods can stain your hands. Break the pods open and push the beans out.

French or dwarf beans – break or cut off the tops and tails. Cut the beans into short pieces if desired.

Runner beans – top and tail as above. Unless very small, runner beans should have the strings sliced from each side before cutting them into diagonal sections.

TO COOK

All beans should be cooked in lightly salted water which is already boiling, for the minimum possible time – no more than 5 minutes. They should still have some 'bite' to them. Better still, steam them for the same time.

BEEF

TO BUY

To roast, choose sirloin or rib of beef. To grill or fry, choose rump, sirloin or fillet steak. For stews and casseroles, choose braising or stewing steak or shin of beef. For burgers, mince dishes or bolognese sauce, choose the best mince you can afford as the cheaper versions tend to include a lot of fat and gristle. Steak mince is the best. (See page 98).

TO STORE

All raw meat should be stored in a refrigerator, for up to 48 hours. Beef can be frozen, but should be tightly wrapped to prevent freezer 'burn'. Freeze joints and steaks for up to 12 months, slices and cubes for up to 8 months, mince for up to 3 months.

TO PREPARE

Roasting joints and steaks may need a little trimming to remove excess fat. Snip through the edging fat on steaks with kitchen scissors at 2 cm (1") intervals to prevent them curling up during cooking. Otherwise, just rinse the meat under cold water and dry with kitchen paper before cooking. To tenderise cuts for quick frying, place the meat between 2 sheets of greaseproof paper and pound it with a heavy object – a heavy saucepan works as well as a meat mallet.

TO COOK

Steaks – whether fried or grilled, cooking steaks properly to the different degrees of doneness involves altering the heat settings as well as the length of cooking time. There is a mistaken idea among people who like rare steaks that people who like them well-done don't care if they are tough, but this is not so. The trick is to start cooking steak at a high temperature, then turn the heat down for the rest of the cooking time, as below. Start by pre-heating the grill or frying pan until it is very hot.

- for a 'blue' (very rare) steak, cook 2 - 2 ½ minutes each side on full heat
- for a rare steak, cook 1 ½ minutes each side on full heat, then 2 minutes each side on medium heat
- for a medium done steak, cook 1 - 1 ½ minutes each side on full heat, then 3 minutes each side on medium heat
- for a well done steak, cook 1 - 1 ½ minutes each side on full heat then 5 - 7 minutes each side on medium heat

To roast a joint of beef, weigh the joint, then preheat the oven to 230°C/450°F/ Gas Mark 8 and start cooking at this temperature. After 15 minutes, turn the oven down to 180°C/350°F/ Gas Mark 4 for the rest of the cooking time.

- for rare meat, total cooking time should be 35 minutes per kg (15 minutes per lb)
- for medium done meat, total cooking time should be 45 minutes per kg (20 minutes per lb)
- for well done meat, total cooking time should be 55 minutes per kg (25 minutes per lb)

During cooking, baste the meat several times with the liquid which collects in the tin. When cooking is complete, transfer the meat to a serving dish, cover it with foil and let it 'rest' for 15 minutes before carving. Provided that you have added no other fat to the pan, you can keep the dripping for frying or spreading on bread. Pour it into a ceramic or glass bowl, let it cool completely, cover it, and it can be kept in the fridge for 2 - 3 weeks.

BEEF STEW

2 kg (4 lbs) shin of beef
or stewing steak
salt and pepper
2 tablespoons plain flour
2 tablespoons olive oil or
50 g (2 oz) beef dripping
350 g (12 oz) onions,
peeled and roughly chopped

450 ml (15 fl oz) beef stock,
or a large tin of plum
tomatoes plus water to make
up to 450 ml
350 g (12 oz) carrots,
peeled and roughly chopped
½ teaspoon dried thyme

Cut the beef into bite-sized chunks and put them in a plastic bag with the flour, salt and pepper and shake the bag until the meat is coated with the seasoned flour. Melt the oil or dripping in a large frying pan and fry the pieces of meat, a few at a time, turning them to brown each side. Transfer the meat to a large saucepan as each batch is done. Add the chopped onions to the frying pan and fry them for a few minutes, then add them to the saucepan. Use a little of the stock to get all the beefy goodness from the frying pan and add that to the saucepan. Finally add the rest of the stock, the carrots and the thyme to the saucepan, bring the contents to the boil, then cover the pan and turn down the heat to let it simmer slowly until the meat is done. This will take about 3 hours. Do not be tempted to turn up the heat for a faster result – these cuts of beef need to cook slowly to release their full potential.

BEETROOT

TO BUY

You can buy beetroot ready cooked, or as raw roots. These should feel firm, and the skins should be intact – damaged roots will 'bleed' out their juice and flavour when you cook them.

TO CLEAN AND PREPARE

Use a soft brush to scrub each root under cold running water, taking care not to damage the skin. Do not cut off the thin part of the root. If there are any leaves still attached, cut the stalks short, but do not cut the top of the root.

TO STORE

Raw beetroot can be stored in a cool dry place for several weeks. Once cooked, store the whole beetroot in the fridge for up to 48 hours – after this time it will start to sweat. Sliced beetroot can be bottled in malt vinegar for those who like it pickled.

TO COOK

Put the whole roots in a large saucepan, cover them with water, add salt and bring to the boil, then simmer for 20 - 30 minutes. Drain and allow to cool before slipping off the skins and slicing or chopping to serve. Alternatively, bake the whole beetroots in the oven at 190°C/375°F/ Gas Mark 5 for 60 - 75 minutes before skinning.

Most people think of beetroot as something to eat cold with a salad, but it is also very tasty served hot. Cook it as above, then skin and slice it while it is still hot before serving it sprinkled with a little brown sugar, or a white sauce (see page 138) into which you have stirred 2 teaspoons of horseradish sauce.

BISCUITS

TO BUY

Unless you are sure of using them all quickly, buy biscuits in small packets, as once opened, they soon lose their crispness.

TO STORE

Store opened packets of biscuits in sealed plastic bags with all the air squeezed out, or in an airtight tin or jar which is only just big enough to hold them all.

TO COOK

Sweet biscuits are quite easy to make at home. This basic biscuit dough can be cut into fancy shapes and left plain or iced after baking. It makes about 16 biscuits. Note that it is important to measure the ingredients accurately.

150 g (6 oz) plain flour   75 g (3 oz) butter
25 g (1 oz) baking powder   1 size 3 egg, beaten
75 g (3 oz) caster sugar

Line two large baking trays with greaseproof paper, and preheat the oven to 180°C/350°F/ Gas Mark 4. Put the dry ingredients into a mixing bowl, cut the butter into small cubes, add it to the mixture and rub it in until the mixture is like fine breadcrumbs. Stir in the egg and mix and knead it in to make a soft dough. Turn this out onto a lightly floured surface and roll it out to about 5mm (¼") thick. Cut out shapes and transfer these to the baking trays, leaving plenty of space between them. Bake for 10 - 12 minutes, until the biscuits are pale golden brown. Let the biscuits cool completely before peeling them off the paper. They can then be stored in an airtight container for up to 3 days.

FLAPJACKS

75 g (3 oz) granulated sugar   150 g (6 oz) rolled oats
75 g (3 oz) butter or margarine   (porridge oats will do)
1 tablespoon golden syrup

Grease a 18cm (7") square baking tin. Preheat the oven to 180°C/350°F/ Gas Mark 4.

Put the sugar, butter and syrup in a saucepan and heat gently, stirring, until the butter has melted. Take the saucepan off the heat and stir in the oats. Spoon the mixture into the baking tin and smooth the top before baking for 25 minutes. Let it cool for a few minutes, then mark it into 16 squares before leaving it to cool completely in the tin. When it is cold, cut right through the marked sections and take them from the tin. Store flapjacks in an airtight box.

BLACKBERRIES

TO BUY

Fresh blackberries should look shiny, feel firm when gently touched, and there should be very little, if any, juice in the bottom of the punnet. You can also pick your own blackberries from the hedgerows in the autumn, but remember that berries found close to a road may be dusty from passing traffic.

TO CLEAN

Blackberries should be rinsed just before use. If there are holes in the bottom of the punnet, rinse the whole punnet under a gently running cold tap, shake off the worst of the water and tip the berries onto double thickness kitchen paper. Check that there are no bits of leaf or other small items sticking to the berries before transferring them to a saucepan to cook. If you intend to use the berries raw, pick out the best specimens and roll them on the paper to dry them off.

TO STORE

Fresh blackberries should not be stored for more than 24 hours, since they start to deteriorate as soon as they are picked. Blackberries can be frozen, either individually or in boxes, but can only be used for cooking, since freezing makes the tissues collapse. Freeze whole berries for up to 12 months, purée for up to 8 months.

TO COOK

Blackberries are mostly liquid, and need hardly any water when cooking. Put 1 - 2 tablespoons of water in the bottom of the pan, add the berries and sugar and set the pan over medium heat. Cover the pan, but check it every couple of minutes to make sure there is sufficient liquid, adding water by the tablespoonful if the pan is dry. You will need about half the weight of sugar to berries, but start with half that amount, as the sweetness of the berries themselves can vary.

If making blackberry and apple pie or crumble (see page 112), cook the two fruits together.

BLACK, RED AND WHITE CURRANTS

TO BUY

Currants are available in mid summer. Red and white currants can be eaten raw, although they can be rather sharp. All should look plump and shiny.

TO STORE

Currants should be eaten or cooked within 2 days of purchase.

TO PREPARE

All currants should be rinsed with cold water. If red and white currants are to be eaten raw or used as a garnish, dry them on kitchen paper. If to be cooked, currants need to be topped and tailed.

TO COOK

Currants need to be gently stewed. They make a lot of juice, so put only a couple of tablespoons of water in the pan to prevent them burning. If you are making jelly, do not crush them while they are cooking, as this makes the jelly cloudy. Weigh the dry currants before you cook them, and add an equal weight of sugar. You may need more sugar, depending on how sharp the currants are, and on your own taste.

BREAD, ROLLS, BREADCRUMBS AND CROÛTONS

TO STORE

Bread can be stored in an airtight box, tin or plastic bag, for several days. It does not need to be stored in the fridge, and should not be stored close to such items as onions, as it may take up the flavour. It can also be frozen for up to 6 months, but crisp crusts of bread or rolls tend to separate after 1 week. For small households, it is most convenient to buy sliced loaves and just take out of the freezer as many slices as you need.

TO MAKE BREADCRUMBS

Use bread which is a couple of days old, removing the crusts. Cut the bread into chunks, and either rub it between your fingers as though making pastry, or put it in a food processor and whizz it until it has reached the texture you want. Use these breadcrumbs within 24 hours, or dry them in a cool oven, spread out in a baking tray. Alternatively, dry the chunks of bread in the oven, then put them in a bag and use a rolling pin to crush them. Store them in an airtight jar for 3 - 4 days.

TO MAKE CROÛTONS

Use bread which is a couple of days old, stacking several slices before cutting off the crusts. Then cut lengthways into strips and finally into cubes. Heat 2 - 3 tablespoons of your preferred oil in a non-stick pan, and toss the cubes of bread until they are brown on all sides. Drain them on kitchen paper and let them cool before using or storing for 2 or 3 days in an airtight jar.

TO MAKE BREAD OR ROLLS

Making yeast bread is quite easy in itself, but kneading is hard work and the rising processes are time consuming. The easiest bread to make is Irish soda bread, which does not need yeast.

IRISH SODA BREAD

450 g (1 lb) plain flour
1 teaspoon salt
½ teaspoon baking soda

1 teaspoon cream of tartar
300 ml (10 fl oz) skimmed milk

Lightly grease a large baking tray and preheat the oven to 220°C/425°F/
Gas Mark 7.

Put the flour, salt, baking soda and cream of tartar in a large bowl. With a
fork, stir well, then gradually stir in most of the milk. Knead with your
hands, adding more milk if necessary. The dough should be easy to handle
but feel soft. Form it into a disc 2 - 3 cm (1") thick and mark it in 8 wedges.

Bake for 30 minutes, before putting the loaf on a wire rack to cool before
serving.

You can use brown flour if you prefer, but may need a little more milk
and another 3 - 5 minutes cooking time.

SIMPLE WHITE BREAD (2 LOAVES)

450 ml (15 fl oz) hand-hot water
1 teaspoon granulated sugar
2 teaspoons dried yeast
700 g (1½ lb) strong white flour,
    plus a little more for kneading

1 teaspoon salt
1 tablespoon olive oil (optional)

You need a warm kitchen to make bread, and a warm place for the dough
to rise. Measure the flour out into a large mixing bowl and leave it to warm
up for 20 minutes or so before starting. Grease two 450 g (1 lb) loaf tins.

Put about a third of the water into a small bowl and stir in the sugar and
yeast. Set aside to froth up for 10 minutes. Add the salt to the flour and
stir it in, then make a well in the centre and pour in the frothed yeast and
oil and the rest of the water. Using your hands, mix everything together
in the bowl, working it until it forms a ball of dough. Turn this out onto
a lightly floured surface and knead it for 10 minutes. It should finally feel
springy and elastic.

Now either return the dough to the mixing bowl and cover it with a clean
cloth, or put it into an oiled plastic bag. Leave it to stand in a warm place
for 1½ hours, or until it has doubled in size. Turn it out onto the floured
surface again and knock the air out – dropping it onto the surface will do
this, or you can punch your fist into it a couple of times. Then knead it
for 5 minutes, divide it into two, shape these into oblongs, put them in
the tins, cover them and leave to rise again for 30 - 60 minutes, until the
dough has risen above the tops of the tins.

While it is rising for the second time, preheat the oven to 230°C/450°F/ Gas Mark 8. Bake the loaves for 35 - 40 minutes, or until they sound hollow when you take them out of the tins and rap the underneath with your knuckles. Take them out of the tins and leave them to cool completely on a wire rack.

To make rolls, follow this recipe, replacing half the water with milk. When you have completed the second knead, divide the dough into 16 pieces, shape each into a round and lay them on a well-greased baking sheet, cover them and leave to rise until they have doubled in size. Preheat the oven to 190°C/375°F/ Gas Mark 5, and bake for 20 - 25 minutes. If you wish, you can paint the top of the rolls with milk and sprinkle them with poppy or sesame seeds before baking.

TEA BREAD

350 g (12 oz) strong white flour	50 g (2 oz) currants
1 teaspoon salt	50 g (2 oz) sultanas
1 teaspoon ground mixed spice	25 g (1 oz) mixed peel
50 g (2 oz) butter	25 g (1 oz) flaked almonds
grated rind of 1 lemon	175 ml (6 fl oz) hand-hot milk
7 g (¼ oz) sachet easy-blend	1 egg, beaten
dried yeast	oil
25 g (1 oz) caster sugar	

Sift the flour, salt and mixed spice into a mixing bowl and rub in the butter. Add the lemon rind, yeast, sugar, currants, sultanas and almonds, peel, and mix them in. Make a well in the middle. Pour in the milk and egg and mix it all to a soft dough, adding a little more milk if needed. Turn the dough out onto a floured surface, flour your hands and knead the dough for 10 minutes, until it feels elastic and smooth. Add more flour to the surface and your hands as necessary to prevent the dough sticking. Lightly oil a large bowl, place the dough into it and cover it with a clean tea-towel or oiled cling-film. Put the bowl in a warm place and leave it for 2 hours, or until the dough has doubled in size.

Flour your hands and the work surface, remove the dough from the bowl and knead it again for 2 minutes. Form it into a rectangle and place it on a greased baking sheet. Make a few shallow diagonal slits across the top with a sharp knife, cover it again as before and leave it in the warm place again for 40-45 minutes or until it has doubled in size. Meanwhile, heat the oven to 190°C/375°F/ Gas Mark 5. When the bread has risen, place it in the middle of the oven and bake for 35-40 minutes. Test it by tapping it with your knuckles. It will sound hollow when done. Put it on a wire rack to cool before serving.

You can use this dough to make hot cross buns. Omit the sultanas and flaked almonds and add 1 teaspoon each of grated nutmeg and ground cinnamon. You will need a little shortcrust pastry for the crosses. After the second knead, divide the dough into 20-24 pieces and form them into a flat-topped ball. Roll out the pastry and cut it into narrow strips to fit the buns. Brush a little beaten egg over the buns, lay a cross of pastry on each and brush more egg on top of the pastry. Cover the buns and leave to rise in a warm place for about 30 minutes or until doubled in size, before baking them at 190°C/375°F/ Gas Mark 5 for 15 minutes. Cool them a little on a wire rack before serving.

BROCCOLI

TO BUY
Fresh broccoli should be firm to the touch and the florets should be dark green. Reject any which feels flabby, or where the florets are turning yellow. You can buy frozen broccoli, but it has very little taste and a poor texture.

TO STORE
Remove any plastic coverings before storage. Keep fresh broccoli in a cool place but not the fridge, as this tends to make it rubbery. Store it for no more than 24 hours before using.

TO PREPARE
The art of preparing broccoli is cutting the stems small enough so that they cook in the same time as the florets. Divide the main head into smaller pieces, each with a small piece of stem, cutting the stems diagonally from just below each floret. Then peel the rest of the stems and cut them into diagonal pieces about 1 cm (½") thick.

TO COOK
Bring a panful of salted water to the boil and drop the broccoli into it. Keep the water at the boil for 5 minutes, then strain the broccoli and serve. Better still, steam the broccoli for 5 - 6 minutes. For a quick meal, toss it with some freshly cooked pasta, or top it with some cheese sauce (see page 138) and pop it under a hot grill for 5 minutes to brown the surface.

Broccoli can also be stir-fried with a little finely chopped chilli pepper or fresh ginger root, and served with noodles or rice.

BRUSSELS SPROUTS

TO BUY

Fresh Brussels sprouts should be deep green. Reject any which are very pale, or showing any yellowing. Choose sprouts which are all more or less the same size. You can buy frozen sprouts, but they have very little taste and a poor texture.

TO CLEAN AND PREPARE

Remove the outer leaves and cut a little piece off the base. Unless the sprouts are very large, there is no need to cut a cross in the base.

TO COOK

Bring a panful of salted water to the boil and drop the sprouts into it. Keep the water at the boil for 5 - 8 minutes, then strain the sprouts and serve. Better still, steam the sprouts for 8 - 10 minutes.

Brussels sprouts can also be shredded and stir-fried, ideally in sesame seed oil.

BUTTER AND MARGARINE

TO BUY

Butter is sold as unsalted, demi-salt, or salted. For cake making and frying, choose unsalted butter. Ghee or clarified butter is ordinary butter which has been heated and strained to remove the solids which can make it go rancid. Butter is made from cream which comes from cows, and all that is ever added to it is salt and, occasionally, yellow colouring.

Margarine is made from oils and fats. Precisely what, in any given case, can be difficult to discover, although some manufacturers do state the origin on the packet. The main advantage of margarine is that some versions can be spread straight from the fridge. Whether or not it is any better for you than butter is questionable – you have to decide for yourself whether you would rather trust cows or chemists.

Some margarines are hydrogenated, which means that they have been through a process which hardens unsaturated oils, but unfortunately, this process also transforms the fat into a saturated fat which is unsuitable for people who are watching their cholesterol. You should also be aware that some margarines made from soya oil may have been made from genetically modified soya beans.

TO STORE

Butter and margarine should be kept in the fridge. It can stay there for several weeks, although the outside surface of butter does sometimes discolour after a while. Butter can also be frozen – unsalted for up to 6 months, salted for up to 3 months. Ghee can be kept in the fridge for 3 - 4 months.

TO CLARIFY BUTTER

Melt the butter very gently in a lipped saucepan such as a milk-pan. As it melts, you will see it separate into liquid fat and fine solids. Turn off the heat and let it stand for a couple of minutes to let the solids settle at the bottom, then carefully pour the liquid into a bowl, discarding the solids. Let it set before covering and storing in the fridge. It can then be used for frying at higher temperatures than ordinary butter without scorching.

TO COOK

Butter and margarine can be used interchangeably when baking, (unless the recipe specifies butter) but not for frying, when only butter will do. You need to watch constantly when frying with unclarified butter, as it can quickly burn and blacken, tainting the food.

CABBAGE

TO BUY

Ball-headed cabbages (Savoy, white cabbage, red cabbage or Chinese cabbage) should feel heavy and firm. Looser cabbage, such as spring cabbage or 'ox-heart' cabbage, or 'spring greens' should have firm leaves which squeak when pressed. Cabbage should not smell sulphurous, or have yellowing leaves. You can also buy other types of oriental greens such as Pak Choi or Bok Choi, which should all feel crisp and have bright leaves and fim stalks.

TO CLEAN AND PREPARE

Ball-headed cabbage - remove any damaged outer leaves, then cut the head in half, then quarters, starting at the stem end. Then either cut into smaller wedges, or remove the tough core and shred the leaves. With Chinese cabbage, there is no core to remove.   Loose cabbage and oriental greens – remove any damaged leaves, trim the stem, and halve or shred it as required.

TO STORE

Remove any plastic coverings before storage. Ball-headed cabbages will keep for several weeks in a cool place. Loose-headed cabbages may be kept for 2 or 3 days.

TO COOK

The unpleasant sulphurous smell which many people associate with boiling cabbage starts about 5 minutes after cooking commences. The trick of cooking cabbage without making the whole house smell is either to cook it very quickly, or to cover the saucepan tightly. In either case, use as little water as possible, but bring the water to the boil before adding the cabbage. Alternatively, steam the cabbage, or put it in a large saucepan with a tablespoon of water and 25 - 50 g (1 - 2 oz) butter, then shake the saucepan while the cabbage cooks. You may need to stir a couple of times, but the whole process should only take about 10 minutes.

Red cabbage needs different treatment, as the leaves are quite tough. The usual way to cook red cabbage is to shred it, then stew it with apple, a little brown sugar and red wine vinegar. For each 450 g (1 lb) of cabbage, add 1 cooking apple, peeled, cored and sliced, 1 tablespoon sugar and 150 ml (5 fl oz) liquid, of which 2 tablespoons should be red wine vinegar or red wine. Bring the liquid to the boil, add the cabbage, bring it back to the boil then turn down the heat and simmer until the cabbage is tender. Some people like to add 1 teaspoon of caraway seeds.

Chinese leaves and oriental greens can be served raw in salads, steamed or stir-fried. Chinese restaurant 'seaweed' isn't seaweed at all, but very finely shredded Savoy cabbage, stir-fried in hot oil until it crisps up.

CAKES

TO STORE

Cakes should be stored in an air-tight tin or plastic box, or can be kept tightly wrapped in kitchen foil or cling-film. Sponge cakes can be frozen, wrapped tightly in foil, for up to 2 months. *Tip*: place the cake on the lid of the tin and put the tin on top, rather than putting the cake into the tin where it might be difficult to remove it.

TO COOK

For success with cakes, it is essential to measure the ingredients accurately. The easiest cake to make is the Victoria sponge.

VICTORIA SPONGE CAKE (serves 8)

175 g (6 oz) butter or
   margarine, softened
175 g (6 oz) caster sugar
3 size 3 eggs, beaten

175 g (6 oz) white self-raising flour
3-4 tablespoons raspberry jam
caster sugar to dredge over the top

Grease two 18 cm (7") sandwich tins. Cut two circles of greaseproof paper using the tin to draw round and use them to line the base of the tins. Preheat the oven to 190°C/375°F/ Gas Mark 5. Put the butter and sugar into a mixing bowl and cream (beat) them together until the mix is pale and creamy-looking. Tip half the flour into the bowl and fold it in with a metal spoon, then repeat with the rest of the flour. Beat in the eggs, a little at a time, then divide the mixture between the prepared tins. Bake for 20 minutes, or until they are light golden-brown on top, feel firm to the touch and are starting to shrink away from the sides of the tins. Turn the sponges out onto a wire rack and leave to cool completely. Remove the greaseproof paper, and spread the jam on one sponge, then turn the other on top of it and press gently to make a sandwich. Dredge the top with a little caster sugar.

To make a chocolate sponge, simply add 2 - 3 tablespoons cocoa powder to the flour and proceed as above.

NOTE: Most cake mixes can be used to make cup-cakes or buns, either in a bun tin with shaped segments, or in paper bun cases. As a rough guide (this will vary slightly with the type of cake mixture) they will need to bake for 10 minutes in an oven set at 200°C/ 400°F/ Gas Mark 6.

CARROTS

TO BUY

Fresh carrots should be firm, unblemished, and dry all over. Big specimens tend to be tough, so always select smaller ones. Young 'new season' carrots, sold in bunches with the leaves on, are sweet and tender, so although you may resent the idea of paying for inedible leaves, they are actually a better buy. You can buy frozen or tinned carrots, but they have very little taste and a poor texture.

TO STORE

Store carrots in a cool dry place for 2 - 3 days. Do not store them in a fridge, as this makes them flabby. If you bought them in a plastic pack, either puncture this or remove it completely, as otherwise the carrots will sweat and start to rot. Remove the leaves from bunches of carrots as they draw the goodness out of the roots.

TO CLEAN AND PREPARE

Young carrots – scrub under cold water, then trim the root end and tops. Older carrots – peel, then cut into long quarters or rondels.

TO SERVE RAW

Raw carrots are a good source of Vitamin A. Young carrots, grated, make a good addition to a salad, or can be cut into sticks and served with dips (see page 67) or on their own (when they may be called 'crudités'). Slimmers should keep a bag of carrot sticks in the fridge for nibbling when hunger strikes.

TO COOK

Young carrots are best steamed for 5 - 6 minutes. Older carrots should be boiled for 8 - 10 minutes, in lightly salted water. Some people like to add ½ teaspoon of sugar to the cooking water.

Boiled with onions in stock, then liquidized, carrots make a quick and tasty soup.

CASSEROLES AND STEWS

Whether cooked in a closed dish (the casserole) in the oven, or in an electric slow-cooker or crockpot, or in a saucepan on top of the stove (when it is known as a stew) the principle is the same – long, slow cooking, which tenderises cheap cuts of meat and blends the flavours of all the ingredients. However, although ideal for cheaper cuts of meat, casseroles can also be made with other cuts or pieces of chicken or other poultry.

TO BUY

The cuts of meat usually associated with casseroles or stews are: flank, leg, shin, shoulder, skirt, or tail (ox-tail) of beef, chuck or blade, or just 'stewing' steak. Middle or scrag end of neck, best end of neck chops or cutlets, or shanks (lower leg) of lamb. Shoulder, spare rib, belly or hand of pork. Older chickens, often labelled 'for boiling'.

TO STORE

Once cooked, casseroles or stews can be kept in the fridge for up to 48 hours, but should be brought back to boiling after 24 hours. They can be frozen for up to 3 months, depending on the ingredients. Potatoes or other root vegetables do not freeze well, so remove them from casseroles before freezing.

TO PREPARE

All excess fat should be removed from the meat, which should then be sealed in hot fat. Some recipes call for the meat to be tossed in plain flour before it is sealed - this is most easily done by putting the flour in a plastic bag, then putting a few pieces of meat in at a time and shaking the bag until they are coated with the flour. Any flour which is left over can be added to the casserole to thicken it. The meat, (and the vegetables,) should be cut to equal-sized pieces so that they cook evenly.

TO COOK

Casseroles – Either bring all the ingredients to boiling point before putting them in the oven, then cook them at a low heat (150°C/300°F/ Gas Mark 2), or start them cooking at a high heat (220°C/425°F/ Gas Mark 7) then turn the heat down to low after about an hour.

Stews – bring the contents of the stewpan to the boil, then cover the pan and turn the heat down to a slow simmer.

Expect casseroles and stews to take at least 3 hours to cook. Then try a piece of meat to see whether it is tender. If not, carry on cooking until it is tender enough for your taste. All casseroles and stews can be cooked in advance and reheated – indeed, some people insist they taste better that way.

CHICKEN CASSEROLE

2 tablespoons olive oil
1½ kg (3 lbs) chicken pieces
  (if you use boneless pieces,
  you will only need 1kg (2 lbs)
12 shallots or button onions,
  peeled
2 sticks celery, roughly chopped

225 g (8 oz) button mushrooms
1 tablespoon plain flour
450 ml (15 fl oz) hot chicken stock
small bunch parsley,
  roughly chopped
  (including the stems)

Preheat the oven to 200°C/400°F/ Gas Mark 6. In a large saucepan, heat the oil and brown the chicken pieces, a few at a time. As each batch is done, drain it and set it aside, then briefly fry the shallots, celery and mushrooms. When all are done, put the flour into the saucepan and stir it into the remains of the oil, then use a little of the stock to mix this into a sauce. Gradually stir in the rest of the stock, add the chicken pieces and bring the whole to the boil. Warm your casserole by rinsing it with hot water. Then transfer all cooked ingredients to the casserole, put the lid on and put it in the oven. Let it cook for 45 minutes, then turn down the heat to 180°C/350°F/ Gas Mark 4, take the casserole out of the oven, add the parsley, then return the casserole to the oven for another 45 minutes to complete cooking.

CAULIFLOWER

TO BUY

Whether white or cream (and sometimes purple or even lime green with pointed florets) the head of cauliflowers should be clean-looking and tightly packed. Reject specimens which are beginning to discolour, or where clumsy leaf-trimming has left cuts in the head, or where the base of the stem is discoloured.

TO STORE

Remove any plastic coverings before storage. Cauliflowers can be kept for 2 or 3 days in a cool dry place.

TO PREPARE

Cut off the leafy base and divide the cauliflower into small pieces, each with a small piece of stem, cutting the stems diagonally from just below each floret. Then peel the rest of the stems and cut them into diagonal pieces about 1 cm (½") thick. (See diagram in broccoli section)

TO COOK

The best way to cook cauliflower is to steam it, for 6 - 8 minutes. Otherwise, cook it in boiling salted water for 5 - 6 minutes, and drain it immediately. Leaving it in cooling water will make it over-cooked and soggy.

Traditionally, cauliflower is served with a plain white sauce or a cheese sauce (see page 138), but it also makes a good vegetable curry, or a raw snack with dips (see page 67).

CURRIED CAULIFLOWER

1 tablespoon vegetable oil	1 medium cauliflower,
1 teaspoon black mustard seeds	trimmed into florets
1 teaspoon turmeric powder	salt
¼ teaspoon chilli powder	3 - 4 tablespoons water
1 small onion, thinly sliced	

In a saucepan, heat the oil, then add the mustard seeds, put a lid on the pan (the mustard seeds will pop and spit) and shake the pan over the heat until you hear the seeds popping. Take the saucepan off the heat until the popping subsides, then remove the lid and stir in the turmeric and chilli powder. Cook for 1 minute, stirring, then add the onion and cook for a further 2 minutes. Then add the cauliflower and shake the pan to coat the cauliflower in the spices before adding salt and the water. Bring the liquid up to boiling, then cover the pan and turn it down to simmer for 5 minutes before serving with boiled rice (and a meat curry if you wish).

If you do not have the individual spices, substitute 2 teaspoons of your preferred strength curry powder.

CELERIAC

TO BUY

Choose specimens which feel hard, and which are not too gnarled underneath.

TO STORE

Celeriac can be stored for several weeks in a cool dry place. Remove any plastic wrapping before storing.

TO CLEAN AND PREPARE

Scrub away any soil adhering to the root end, then use a heavy knife to cut off this end. Peel the whole thing thickly and cut it into chunks (for mash) or slices and then thin strips (for salads). Drop each piece into acidulated water (see page 5) to prevent discolouration.

TO COOK

For salads – blanch the strips. Squeeze the juice of half a lemon into a saucepan of boiling water, drop the strips into the water and bring the water back to the boil. As soon as it is boiling, drain the celeriac and cool it by rinsing it under cold running water. Drain thoroughly before dressing with mayonnaise or vinaigrette.

For mash or gratins – cook chunks in simmering water until tender. This will take the same time as cooking potato. Drain and mash, either on its own, or with potato.

CELERY

TO BUY

The most flavoursome celery is English. This is available in early winter, and will be labelled 'Fenland' or 'Lincolnshire' celery. Imported celery is available throughout the year, and may be white or green. Choose specimens which have tight stems and feel heavy.

TO CLEAN

English celery may have black soil adhering to it. Wash this off, using a soft brush if necessary.

TO STORE

Celery can be kept for up to a week, and will remain fresh if you stand the head up in a jar with a little water in the bottom. You can remove outer leaves to use and return the rest to the jar. Change the water every day.

TO PREPARE

Outer stalks should have the tough strings stripped out, and are best used in stews or soup. For eating raw, just separate the stems and serve them standing upright in a jar or tall glass. Cut the heart into halves or quarters, leaving some of the root end attached to each piece.

TO COOK

Celery hearts can be braised to serve as a vegetable accompanying meat or poultry. Remove the outer leaves and base of the heart, then cut the heart in half or quarters. Blanch these in boiling water for 3 - 5 minutes, then drain but retain the cooking water. Place the hearts in an ovenproof dish, season with salt and pepper, add a few dabs of butter and sufficient of the cooking water to cover them before baking in a medium oven for about 30 minutes. Drain the hearts and put them on a serving dish, then use the cooking liquid to make a white or cheese sauce.

CHARCUTERIE AND COOKED MEATS

TO BUY

There is such a wide range of cooked meat products on sale that what you buy is very much a matter of individual taste. Choose from:
- salami and other similar sausages, ready sliced or sliced as you want, to eat as they are.
- liver sausage, which can be used in sandwiches, or fried.
- black pudding (a sausage made mainly from blood) which is usually fried.
- slices from joints – beef, ham, pork, turkey, either plain or fancy, according to your taste. You can sometimes buy 'end' pieces to cut yourself, which are considerably cheaper than tidy slices.
- reconstituted meats, such as 'ham' or 'chicken' slices. These are not slices from a joint or whole chicken breast, but are made up of meat which has been minced and then pressed together into a block for slicing. Although convenient for making sandwiches, the texture of these can be unpleasant, and they are not necessarily cheaper than the real thing.

TO STORE

All meats bought from a delicatessen counter should be eaten within 48 hours. Some pre-packed meats can be kept longer – check the 'use by' dates on the pack. All should be kept in the fridge.

CHEESE

TO BUY

For grating, buy hard cheeses such as Cheddar or Gruyère. For melting, buy either hard cheeses, or softer cheeses such as Emmenthal or Mozarella. For all other purposes, buy what you like the taste of! Buy only as much as you will use in a week, as cheese does not keep indefinitely. Two things you should be aware of when buying cheese - cheese made from unpasteurised milk should not be eaten by the very old, the very young, or pregnant women; and that some cheeses contain rennet, which is made from the inside of calves' stomachs, and thus unsuitable for vegetarians.

TO STORE

Hard cheeses can be frozen, either whole or grated, for up to 3 months. Other cheese should be stored in a cool place or a fridge, in a covered dish or tightly wrapped in foil. Remove any plastic wrappings, as these make the cheese greasy. Soft cheeses such as Brie or Camembert should be taken out of the fridge at least 24 hours before eating.

TO COOK

Cheese should be cooked gently, as too high a heat or over-cooking will make it separate into liquid grease and a substance with the texture of rubber.

WELSH RAREBIT

This classic savoury dish can be made with various cheeses, including Cheddar, Cheshire, or Double Gloucester, and once the basic sauce has been made, it can be kept, covered, in the fridge for up to 3 days. To ring the changes, it can be served topped with a poached egg, or slices of ham.

25 g (1 oz) butter
25 g (1 oz) plain flour
1 teaspoon mustard powder
(or made mustard)
4 tablespoons milk

4 tablespoons beer (optional – if not available, use more milk)
350-450 g (12oz-1lb) grated cheese
salt and white pepper
8 slices toast, spread thinly with butter

Melt the butter in a saucepan, then stir in the flour and mustard and cook gently for 2 minutes before gradually stirring in the milk, then the beer. Gradually stir in the cheese and continue to stir while it melts into the sauce. Taste and season. Take the saucepan off the heat. Spread the sauce thickly over the toast and grill until the top is golden and bubbling. Serve straight away.

For a quicker cheesy snack, **make cheese on toast.** For each slice of buttered toast you will need 25 g (1 oz) sliced cheese, which you lay on the toast before putting it under the grill until it bubbles. Some people like to sprinkle the cheese with paprika or cayenne pepper before grilling, or to spread a little Marmite or sandwich pickle on the toast before adding the cheese.

CHERRIES

TO BUY

Cooking or Morello cherries are very dark when ripe. Dessert cherries can be yellowish-pink (called 'white'), red or very dark red ('black'). All should feel firm, have shiny skins and a fruity smell. Select your own cherries whenever possible, and choose the ones with their stalks still on, as pulling the stalks off bruises the flesh.

Tinned or bottled cherries are a good buy for making pies.

TO CLEAN

Rinse under the cold tap just before serving or cooking. Dry by rolling them gently on kitchen towel.

TO STORE

Fresh cherries can be kept for 2 - 3 days in the fridge, or in a fruit bowl at room temperature. Dessert cherries should not be frozen, but Morello cherries do not suffer a loss of taste if frozen raw and with their stones left in. Freeze them for up to 12 months.

TO COOK

You can cook Morello or dessert cherries. If diners don't mind spitting out the pips, leaving them in does give a slightly better flavour. To remove the stones before cooking, you will need a cherry stoner. This is best done with stoner and cherry inside a plastic bag, as the juice tends to spurt and can stain.

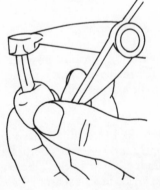

Either gently poach the cherries in a saucepan with a little sugar and water, or put them in a baking dish and bake at 190°C/375°F/ Gas Mark 5 for 20 - 30 minutes. For each 450 g (1 lb) cherries, you will need approximately 150 g (6 oz) sugar.

CHESTNUTS

TO BUY

Fresh chestnuts are available from early winter, but you need to be sure they are this year's crop. The skins should be shiny and supple, and the nut should fill the skin. Reject any which are dull, feel brittle, or where the nut has shrunken away from the skin – or where there are any holes in the skin (evidence of maggots). Fresh chestnuts are time-consuming and fiddley to deal with, so unless you want them to roast and eat straight from the skin, it might be better to buy them frozen, vacuum-packed, or dried. Chestnut purée is also available in tins, but check that you are not buying sweet purée if you want it for soups.

TO CLEAN AND PREPARE

Frozen chestnuts need only to be thawed. Vacuum-packed nuts need no preparation. Dried nuts should be soaked for several hours in warm water, then picked over for any odd bits of skin. Fresh nuts, whether to be boiled or roasted, should have the skins punctured to prevent them exploding during cooking. (This is particularly important if you intend to microwave them.) The easiest way to puncture the skin is to cut a cross through the pointed end.

TO STORE

Fresh chestnuts can be kept in a cool dry place for several weeks, but you should check them regularly to make sure they aren't drying out. Cooked chestnuts can be frozen for up to 6 months. Peel them, open freeze them, then bag them up.

TO COOK

To oven-roast chestnuts, place them in a baking tray or roasting tin and put them in the oven at 220°C/425°F/ Gas Mark 8 for 30 - 40 minutes. To roast chestnuts over an open fire, put them in a long-handled frying pan and roast them for 10 - 15 minutes, shaking the pan at regular intervals. To boil, simply put the nuts in a saucepan of boiling water, bring the water back to the boil and cook for 5 minutes until the outer and inner skin comes off easily. Use an old saucepan, as the colour comes out of the skins and can discolour the pan. Chestnuts are easiest to peel when they are hot, so cook them in small batches.

After skinning, whole chestnuts can be boiled for a further 5 minutes to add to Brussels sprouts, or for 10 minutes to mash for stuffing turkeys. They can also be added to beef stews.

CHICKEN

TO BUY

Fresh whole chickens for roasting should have moist skin and plump breasts. Calculate the size of bird (frozen or fresh) to buy at a rate of 450 g (1 lb) per person. Choose an 'oven-ready' bird if possible. Otherwise, ask the butcher to remove the head and feet. You can also buy various cuts of chicken, in which case you will need 150 - 225 g (6 - 8 oz) per person. It is well worth buying whole fresh chickens and jointing them yourself to freeze. Free-range chickens usually have the best flavour. Buy organic if you are concerned about chemicals and hormones.

TO CLEAN

With whole birds, always look inside the cavity – there may be a packet of giblets in there. If so, remove it before rinsing the bird under cold running water. Joints should also be rinsed under cold water before cooking. Use the giblets to make a stock for gravy.

TO STORE

Fresh chicken should be kept in a fridge or cool larder for no more than 48 hours before cooking. Frozen raw chicken should never be refrozen after thawing. Freeze chicken portions for up to 12 months.

TO PREPARE

Frozen birds must be completely defrosted before cooking to avoid the risk of salmonella. This will take a minimum of 8 hours at room temperature or 24 hours in a refrigerator. Large birds will take a lot longer.

Oven-ready birds need only to be wiped over with kitchen paper, and stuffed (if desired) before roasting. Others should have the cavity wiped out as well before stuffing and trussing. To truss a chicken, you will need skewers or kitchen string. Turn the bird breast side down, and pull the flap of skin over the neck cavity and across the backbone. Twist the wings so that the tips cross this flap and hold it in place. Turn the bird and arrange the legs so that they are tucked in against the sides of the breast, with the foot end nearest the pointed end of the breast. Use the skewers or string to fasten the bird in this position before roasting.

TO COOK

To roast a whole chicken, preheat the oven to 200°C/400°F/Gas Mark 6. Place the bird in a roasting tin, and roast it for 30 minutes. Baste it with the fat from the tin, then continue cooking for up to 1 hour, depending on the size. Check for doneness by sticking a sharp knife into the thigh – the juice should run clear. Pieces of chicken – quarters, breasts, thighs, drumsticks or wings, can also be roasted.

Some pieces, especially breasts, can be grilled or barbecued. Skinned breast can be sliced and fried or stir-fried. Pieces, and whole chickens, can also be steamed or stewed. In fact, you can cook chicken almost any way, as long as you cook it well to avoid the risk of salmonella poisoning.

CHICORY AND ENDIVE

TO BUY
Chicory comes in two forms – blanched 'chicons' of tightly packed bitter leaves, and looser heads of leaves for salads. The best known of the latter is the red chicory known as 'radicchio'. Endive is either broad leaved or frizzy leaved, and can be bought either as heads (with the centre blanched) or trimmed and packed as loose leaves.

TO STORE
All types of chicory or endive should be kept in the fridge, for 3 - 4 days. Check the packet for keeping times on ready prepared leaves.

TO CLEAN AND PREPARE
Chicons should have any discoloured outer leaves removed, and a thin slice removed from the bottom. For salads, the leaves can be shredded, or the larger leaves can be removed and filled with chopped eggs, cream cheese, etc.

TO COOK
Chicory can be braised to serve as a vegetable with meat or poultry. Leave the chicons whole, then follow the instructions for braising celery hearts (see page 54), checking for doneness after 20 minutes.

CHIPS

TO BUY
You can buy frozen chips, either to fry or to cook in the oven, but these are much more expensive, and never quite as nice, as real chips made from real potatoes. Choose the right sort of potato – Cara, Desiree, Wilja, or Maris Piper, for the best results.

TO PREPARE
The larger you cut the chips, the less fat any given amount of potato will absorb. Leaving the skin on the potato will also reduce the fat absorption. Scrub the potatoes clean, and peel them if desired, then slice them thickly and finally cut them into chips. If you like them crinkle-cut, you can buy a special cutter. After cutting, rinse the chips in cold water (if you have

time, leave them to soak for 30 minutes) and dry them on a clean tea-towel before cooking.

TO COOK

To deep-fry chips, use lard, or a good quality sunflower or peanut oil. The oil should be heated to 190°C/375°F before the chips go in. If your fryer does not have a temperature gauge, toss in a cube of bread. This should cook to golden brown when the fat is at the right temperature. Don't try to cook too many chips in one batch, as this will reduce the temperature of the oil and the chips will end up soggy. Put the raw chips in the basket and lower it into the oil, then cook the chips for 5 minutes, then pull the basket out and wait for a couple of minutes while the oil heats up again before lowering the basket to cook the chips for a further 2 - 3 minutes. This will give you chips which are cooked right through and crisp on the outside without being soggy in the middle. Drain well, first over the pan, then by tossing on kitchen paper before serving.

To oven-cook chips, cut, rinse and dry the chips, then toss them in a bowl with some salt and oil - you'll need 3 tablespoons for 450 g (1 lb) chips. Preheat the oven to 220°C/424°F/ Gas Mark 7. Spread the chips in a roasting tin and bake for 40 - 45 minutes, shaking and turning them at least twice. Drain them on kitchen paper before serving.

COCONUT

TO BUY

Coconut comes in various forms – whole nuts, dried flesh in shreds (dessicated coconut) or thin swirls for decoration, and the liquid extracted from the flesh which comes in tins, solid blocks, or powder. These will be called coconut milk or coconut cream, but should not be confused with the liquid that can sometimes be found inside a whole nut. Although purists insist that you should use the flesh from a whole nut, they are a major task to open and prepare, and for most purposes the dried or creamed versions work just as well.

When buying whole nuts, make sure that the shell is not cracked and that the 'eyes' look solid and dry. Hold the nut close to your ear and shake it gently to listen for liquid sloshing about inside - this tells you that the flesh will be desirably moist.

TO STORE

Whole coconuts will keep for many months. Once opened, the flesh will dry out unless you wrap it in clingfilm. Dried flesh will keep for 5 - 6 weeks in an airtight container, as will dried milk or opened blocks of solid cream. Tinned milk or cream should be used within 3 days of opening.

TO PREPARE

Coconut 'milk' is not the clear liquid inside the whole nut, but an extract which you make from the grated flesh. Start with a whole coconut. Pierce the eyes and pour out the liquid (some people like to drink it) then put the nut into a plastic bag and hit it with a hammer to break it open and extract the flesh then remove the brown skin with a vegetable peeler before grating the flesh finely. Place it in a large bowl, then cover it with boiling water. Stir well, then leave it to steep for 30 minutes. Place a sieve over a clean bowl, double a large piece of butter muslin and lay it over the sieve, then pour the steeped coconut in. When most of the liquid has run through, gather up the edges of the muslin and squeeze out the rest of the liquid. Discard the grated flesh.

THAI COCONUT MILK SOUP

This soup is so delicious that it is worth going out of your way to buy the fresh galangal (which looks like a smaller version of ginger root), lemon grass and Kaffir lime leaves.

1 tablespoon vegetable oil
1 small onion, thinly sliced
1 tablespoon Thai fish
   sauce (nam pla)
1 chicken breast, skinned
   and thinly sliced across the grain
1 block (or 1 tin) coconut cream,
   broken into small pieces

1 litre (2 pts) water
2 stalks fresh lemon grass,
   finely sliced
50 g (2 oz) fresh galangal,
   finely sliced
6 kaffir lime leaves, finely shredded
2 fresh hot chilli, finely sliced
   (optional)

In a large saucepan, heat the oil and fry the onion until it is translucent. Add the fish sauce and chicken and fry for a moment, then add the coconut cream and water, lemon grass, galangal, lime leaves and chilli. Bring the soup slowly to the boil, then turn down and simmer for 5 minutes. Serve as a soup, or strain, serve the liquid as a soup and the solids on boiled rice.

CORN ON THE COB

TO BUY

Buy only as much fresh corn as you intend to eat that day, selecting plump cobs with moist-feeling husks. The sugar in corn starts to turn to starch as soon as the cobs are picked, and the kernels get progressively tougher as time goes by.

TO PREPARE

Pull the husks and silky threads off each cob, then trim the tip and stem end. Put each cob in cold water while you deal with the rest.

TO STORE
To freeze fresh corn, blanch it as soon as you get home, then let it cool before freezing for up to 12 months.

TO COOK
Put the cobs in salted boiling water and boil them for 8 - 10 minutes. Drain and serve straightaway.

To cook corn on a barbecue, don't remove the husks or silks. Immerse the cobs in cold water for at least an hour before cooking, then drain them well and put them on the barbecue grill for 10 - 15 minutes, turning them once or twice. The moisture in the husks will effectively steam the corn.

Frozen corn can be cooked straight from the freezer. Drop the cobs in boiling water as above, then cook for 10 - 12 minutes.

TO PREPARE YOUR OWN SWEETCORN
To get sweetcorn off the cob, either use very fresh raw corn, or first cook the cobs, (saving the cooking water) then hold each one upright on a chopping board and use a sharp knife to scrape downwards. Turn the cob as you work until all the kernels are off. Then drop the scraped cobs back into the cooking water and return them to the boil for 5 - 10 minutes, to extract the last of the goodness from them. Remove the cobs and throw them away. The liquid is now a good base for sweetcorn soup, or as a general vegetable stock.

See also Sweetcorn (page 150).

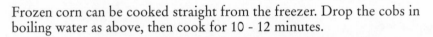

COURGETTES

TO BUY
Courgettes should be rigid, with shiny skin. The smaller they are, the better the texture and flavour. Reject over-large specimens and those which are flabby and bendy. Buy only as many as you need, as they deteriorate quickly. You can also buy a flat type of courgette called 'pattypan', which are sold in packs in larger supermarkets.

TO CLEAN AND PREPARE
Wipe over with a damp cloth and trim off the tip and stem end. There is no need to peel courgettes. For some recipes, and with larger specimens, you may need to degorge them.

TO COOK

Whole courgettes can be boiled, ideally for no more than 5 minutes. It is better to steam them, either whole or cut into chunks, for 4 - 5 minutes. They can also be sliced thinly and fried, as they are or dipped into a thin batter.

Really fresh baby courgettes can also be sliced and eaten raw in a salad instead of cucumber.

CRABS

TO BUY

Unless you live close to the sea, crabs are sold ready cooked. They should feel heavy for their size. You can buy separate claws as well as whole crabs.

TO STORE

Crab may be kept in the fridge for no more than 24 hours, or up to 1 month in the freezer.

TO PREPARE

Pull off the legs and claws. Crack these open with a small hammer or nut-crackers and extract the meat with a fine skewer or fine-bladed knife. Place the body of the crab on its back on a chopping board and pull off and discard the tail flap. Stand the body on edge and use your thumbs to push the main body chamber from the shell. Pull off and discard the greyish gills (called 'dead mens fingers') and the stomach sac. Use a sharp

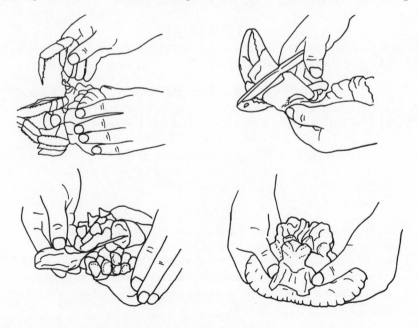

knife to split the body into smaller pieces and use a small skewer and teaspoon to prise off the white meat. Now use a spoon to remove the darker meat and any coral from inside the shell, keeping this separate from the white meat. This dark meat is stronger flavoured and normally served separated from the white.

If you intend to serve the meat in the shell, use a small hammer or pliers to break the underside of the shell back to the rim, before rinsing it out and drying it. Season the two sets of meat with salt, black or cayenne pepper and lemon juice, shredding the meat if necessary. Pack the meat back into the shell, with the white meat on each side and the dark meat down the middle.

CREAM

TO BUY

Cream is designated into types which differ in butterfat content, not, as many people think, thickness. Half-cream and single cream have the lowest butterfat content, and cannot be whipped. Whipping cream comes next, and should double its volume when whipped. Double cream can be poured or whipped. Clotted cream is very thick and can be spread on scones or used to garnish desserts. You can also buy soured cream, or crème fraîche, for savoury recipes. (You can make your own sour cream by adding lemon juice to fresh cream – you'll need 1 tablespoon fresh lemon juice for each 600 ml [1 pint] carton of cream.)

TO STORE

Cream should be stored in the fridge, for 3 - 4 days. Once opened, it should be used within 2 days.

TO WHIP CREAM

Whipping cream works best when the cream, bowl, and whisk are all chilled. Use either a hand balloon whisk or electric beater. Start slowly until you can see how the cream is behaving (this can vary considerably), then fast until it starts to thicken, then slowly again until it reaches the stage you want. Never leave an electric beater running and go away, as you may come back to find you have butter!

TO COOK WITH CREAM

Many recipes such as soups call for cream to be added towards the end of cooking. Always take the pan from the heat and let it cool slightly before adding the cream, as otherwise it may curdle. Double cream is less likely to curdle. When the dish contains acidy ingredients such as wine or lemon juice, it is best to let the mixture cool down, then add the cream and reheat gently to serving heat.

SYLLABUB

This is an old dessert which is very quick and easy to prepare.

150 ml (5 fl oz) double or
  whipping cream
90 ml (3 fl oz) white wine

50 g (2 oz) caster sugar
juice of ½ lemon
lemon zest for garnishing

Cool all the ingredients. Put everything except the lemon zest into a bowl and whisk it until it is quite stiff. Spoon it into 4 bowls or decorative glasses and chill for 1 - 3 hours. Garnish with the lemon zest before serving.

CUCUMBER

TO BUY

Cucumbers should have unblemished shiny dark green skin, and feel firm. Reject specimens which feel flabby or are turning yellow. You can sometimes buy mini cucumbers, or halves – just do the arithmetic to see whether they are good value.

TO STORE

Cucumbers can be kept in the salad drawer in the fridge for up to a week.

TO PREPARE

Whether or not you peel cucumbers for salads is a matter of taste. Some people find the skin indigestible, others don't. Equally, some salad dishes such as cucumber and yoghurt salad require the cucumber to be degorged. If you want to remove the seeds from a cucumber, cut it in half lengthways, then run a teaspoon down the centre to scoop out the seeds.

TO COOK

Cucumbers can be baked or braised, (with or without stuffing) or stir fried. In all cases, remove the peel, cut the cucumber into thick slices (or halves with the seeds removed) and degorge before cooking.

CUCUMBER SANDWICHES

To make cucumber sandwiches you need thinly sliced bread (white or brown, according to taste), very soft butter, and very thinly sliced, peeled cucumber. A little white pepper is optional. The crusts should always be removed, and the sandwiches cut into dainty triangles.

CUCUMBER SALAD (Tzatziki)

1 large cucumber
1 teaspoon salt
2 garlic cloves (optional)
600 ml (1 pt) plain yoghurt

black pepper
1 tablespoon finely chopped
   fresh mint leaves

Peel the cucumber, slice it thinly and spread the slices out on a large plate, then sprinkle the salt over them and leave them to degorge for 20 minutes. Transfer the slices to a colander, rinse them under running water and shake them well to get rid of as much water as you can. If using the garlic, peel the cloves and crush them well, then stir them into the yoghurt. Add the cucumber slices to the yoghurt, sprinkle generously with the pepper, stir in the mint and transfer the whole mixture to a serving dish. It tastes best if allowed to chill in the fridge for a couple of hours before serving.

You can also use this salad for a dip if you chop the cucumber finely instead of slicing it.

CUSTARD

This is not the stuff you make from packets of powder, but the real thing, made with eggs and milk. It is almost as easy as the packet version, but tastes far superior. As well as being used for pouring over fruit pies, it can be used to make many other puddings such as real trifle.

600 ml (1 pt) milk
3 - 4 drops vanilla essence
   (or vanilla pod – see below)

2 whole eggs plus 4 yolks
25 g (1 oz) caster sugar

Heat the milk and vanilla to just below boiling point, then take it off the heat and allow it to cool for a few minutes. Meanwhile, beat the eggs, yolks, and sugar together. Pour the milk slowly onto the egg mixture, whisking as you pour. Either wash up the milk saucepan before you re-use it, or use a clean one, preferably with a heavy base. Pour the mixture into this clean saucepan and cook it over a gentle heat, stirring constantly until it thickens. Do not let it boil or it will curdle. When it is as thick as you want it, transfer it to a jug for serving hot or cold.

To prevent a skin forming while the custard cools, cut out a piece of greaseproof paper to fit the jug and press this onto the surface, removing it before serving. Cold custard can be kept in the fridge for up to 48 hours. For an even better flavour, omit the vanilla essense and use a vanilla pod. Put the pod into the saucepan with the milk and bring it to just below boiling point, then turn off the heat and leave the milk to infuse for 10 - 15 minutes before straining it and carrying on as above. Rinse the vanilla pod in clean water and dry it carefully before storing it to use again. You can use each vanilla pod this way four or five times.

REAL TRIFLE

1 recipe custard, as above
6 trifle sponges
raspberry (or strawberry) jam
225g (8 oz) fresh or frozen
   raspberries (or strawberries)

2 glasses medium or sweet sherry
275 ml (10 fl oz) double cream,
   whipped to soft peaks
50 g (2 oz) flaked almonds or
   hazelnuts, toasted

Make the custard and leave it to cool. Slice the trifle sponges in half and spread them with the jam (use the same jam as fruit). Fit them into the bottom of a large serving bowl (traditionally a glass bowl), cutting them to fit if necessary. Spread the fruit on top, cutting large fresh strawberries into smaller pieces, and adding the juice if you are using frozen fruit. Pour the sherry over this layer and leave it to soak in before pouring the custard on top. Add the whipped cream and finally sprinkle the nuts over the top. Chill for 2 - 3 hours before serving.

DIPS

You can buy dips to serve as starters with batons of raw vegetables, pitta bread or crisp biscuits, but it is very easy to make your own. All you have to do is assemble the ingredients and mash or process them together to a thick creamy consistency. All dips should be stored in the fridge and with the exception of olive dips, should be consumed within 24 hours of making. Olive based dips can be stored for up to a week if you add a layer of olive oil to the top of the pot (stir this in before using).

YOGHURT, SOUR CREAM, OR CREAM CHEESE BASED DIPS

The simplest dip of all is yoghurt with a little lemon juice stirred in (1 teaspoon lemon juice per small pot yoghurt). Vary this by adding mashed avocado, mashed blue cheese, mashed anchovies, curry powder, tomato purée, or chopped onion, nuts or fresh herbs.

BEAN BASED DIPS

Start with a tin of cooked beans (red kidney, haricot, etc) drain the beans and process them with your choice of chopped onion, lemon juice, olive oil, honey, chilli pepper, garlic, Worcestershire sauce or fresh herbs.

OLIVE BASED DIPS

Start with stoned olives (green or black), add some good quality olive oil, garlic and fresh or dried thyme and oregano, plus, if you wish, anchovies.

HUMMUS

This classic dip is made of chick peas, and is usually served with warm pitta bread.

1 x 420 g tin of chick peas
2 - 4 cloves garlic
1 tablespoon sesame seed paste
   (also called Tahini) – optional

olive oil, salt, lemon juice
1 teaspoon chopped parsley
   to garnish

Drain the peas but reserve the liquid from the tin. (You can remove the skins from the peas, but it isn't really necessary.) Put the peas and garlic in a liquidizer or food processor and whizz them until they are fine, then gradually add the sesame seed paste (if using it) and oil until you have a thick paste. To thin, if you wish, use a little of the liquid from the tin. Add lemon juice and salt to your taste. Transfer the hummus to a serving bowl and sprinkle the chopped parsley on top.
See also Aubergine Caviare (page 30) and Guacamole (page 31).

DRIED FRUIT

TO BUY

Most supermarkets will stock the various forms of dried grape (currants, raisins, sultanas) and a selection of other dried fruit such as prunes, dates, apricots and figs. Health food stores will have a larger selection which could include apples, pears, peaches, pineapple and mangoes. Where dried grapes are concerned, if you use a lot, it is more economic to buy sultanas (the most expensive) and use them for everything, than to keep packets of all three types in your store cupboard.

TO STORE

Unopened packets can be kept in a cupboard for up to 1 year. Once opened (or bought loose) dried fruit should be kept in an airtight container, for up to 6 months.

TO PREPARE

Dried fruit bought in packets from reputable suppliers can be eaten straight from the packet as snacks or used in recipes without rinsing. Otherwise, it should be rinsed for eating uncooked or using in cakes, and the soaking water when it has been soaked should be thrown away. To soak and plump up dried fruit, separate the individual fruits, put them in a large bowl and fill the bowl with boiling water, then leave it to stand for 5 - 10 minutes for grapes, 45 - 50 minutes for other fruit. Dried apples and pears may need longer.

For special puddings, or just to spoon over a serving of ice cream, you might like to keep a jar of sultanas soaking in brandy.

DUCK

TO BUY

Oven-ready whole ducks can be bought fresh or frozen. Duck breasts are a good buy if you do not want to bother with a whole bird.

TO CLEAN, AND STORE

See chicken (page 58)

TO PREPARE

Proceed as for chicken (page 58) until the bird is trussed, then prick the skin all over with a sharp skewer. This helps the fat to run off during cooking. You can rub the skin with salt and pepper if you wish.

TO COOK

To roast a whole duck, preheat the oven to 200°C/400°F/Gas Mark 6. Place the bird, breast downwards, on a rack in a roasting tin, and roast it for 30 minutes. Turn the bird breast side up and roast it for a further 25 minutes. Baste it with the fat from the tin, then turn the oven down to 180°C/350°F/Gas Mark 4 and cook it for a further 1 ½ to 2 hours. Save the fat from the tin to use for frying. NB: whole ducks require 40 to 60 minutes per Kilo (20 - 30 minutes per lb) depending on how you like your meat.

DUCK BREASTS WITH ORANGE SAUCE

25 g (1 oz) saltless butter
1 tablespoon olive oil
2 duck breasts (sometimes called 'magrets')
zest and juice from 2 juicy oranges with unblemished skin

1 level tablespoon plain flour
2 tablespoons medium sherry
2 teaspoons brown sugar
salt and pepper

Heat the butter and oil in a frying pan and fry the duck breasts for 10 - 15 minutes each side, starting skin side down.

Meanwhile, use a zester to remove as much as you can of the zest from the oranges and reserve this in a bowl with the juice of the oranges. When the duck breasts are cooked, transfer them to plates and put them in a warm oven to keep hot while you make the sauce.

Stir the flour into the fat in the frying pan, then gradually stir in the juice and zest from the oranges, the sherry and the sugar. Cook, stirring, for 2 - 3 minutes, then taste and season. Pour the sauce over the duck breasts and serve with fresh green peas.

EGGS

NOTE

The young, the elderly, pregnant women and people with immune deficiencies should not eat dishes which contain raw or partially cooked eggs, due to the risk of salmonella.

TO BUY

Eggs come in various sizes, either numbered (1 is the biggest) or 'large', 'medium' and 'small'. Unless otherwise stated, recipes in this and other cookery books intend you to use a medium (size 3) egg. Hens eggs can have white or brown shells. The food content of the eggs is the same, regardless of shell colour. Ducks eggs may have bluey-green shells, and are richer tasting than hens eggs. They are particularly good for cake making.

To test whether an egg is fresh, place it in a glass of water – if it sinks, it is fresh, if it floats, it isn't.

TO STORE

Raw eggs should be stored for no more than 18 days from laying, with their large end upwards, in a fridge. Leave them in the carton, as they can pick up taste and smell from other items in the fridge. Eggs cook more evenly at room temperature, so take them out of the fridge 30 minutes in advance of cooking. Separated yolks or whites can be stored in the fridge for up to three days, as long as they are covered with a layer of water to prevent their drying out. They can also be frozen, but should be thawed in the fridge overnight before use. Cooked egg dishes should be allowed to cool completely, then refrigerated.

TO PREPARE

To break an egg, take it in one hand and tap it sharply on a hard surface until one side of the shell is broken (a blunt surface such as the edge of a bowl is best as this is less likely to break the yolk). Then push your thumb on the crack and use your other hand to pull the egg apart over a bowl. Break each egg into a small bowl to check that it is OK before you add it to the other ingredients.

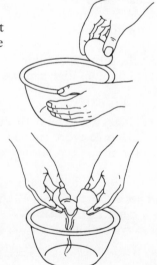

'Separating' an egg means separating the yolk from the white. There are several ways you can do this. (Passing the yolk from one half of the shell to the other, and letting the white fall into a bowl is not recommended, as there is a risk of bacterial contamination.)

- break the egg and tip the contents into your hand, letting the white run out between your fingers into a bowl.
- break the egg into a funnel or a perforated spoon and let the white run through.
- break the egg onto a saucer, then place an egg-cup over the yolk and hold it there while you pour the white into a bowl.

NB – if you intend to whip the whites, make sure the bowl into which you put them is scrupulously clean, and take care no yolk escapes into that bowl, or you may have difficulty whipping the whites.

TO COOK

BOILED EGGS
For a soft egg, boil it for 3-4 minutes. For a hard egg, boil it for 8-10 minutes. In either case, the timing starts when the water boils. To prevent cracking, put the eggs in warm water in a saucepan and then bring the water up to the boil. If they do crack, add some salt to the water to prevent too much white escaping.

FRIED EGGS
To fry eggs, heat the fat before adding the eggs, then turn the heat down to medium, or you risk ending up with tough whites. (Don't add salt during cooking, as this also makes the whites tough.) For the best shape, fry each egg separately, or the whites will run together. For people who like their eggs turned, use a small spoon or bulb baster to pour hot fat over the top of the egg while the bottom cooks, then when the top of the yolk has just set, use a spatula to turn the egg over. Eggs need about 1 minute per side to cook. You can use butter, bacon fat, or oil to fry eggs, and you'll need about 1 tablespoon of fat for each egg.

POACHED EGGS
You don't need an egg poacher to poach eggs. Just half-fill a frying pan or wide saucepan with boiling water, add a teaspoon of vinegar, turn the water down to simmer, break the eggs and carefully slide them into the water one by one. Leave them to cook for 4 - 6 minutes, depending on how well you like them done, then lift them out with a slotted spoon to serve.

BAKED OR CODDLED EGGS
For each egg you will need a ramekin or other small dish. Butter the dish generously, then break the egg into it. You can put 2 teaspoons of lightly fried mushrooms or cooked spinach in the bottom of the dish if you like, or sprinkle chopped chives, cayenne or paprika, grated cheese or just black pepper on top. Wrap the dishes in foil, then place them in a baking dish, pour in boiling water to reach halfway up the dishes, then bake them at 190°C/375°F/ Gas Mark 5 for 7 - 10 minutes.

OMELETTES (per person)

2-3 eggs

salt

pepper

butter for the pan

Break the eggs into a bowl and beat them enough to mix well. Season to taste. In an omelette pan or non-stick frying pan, melt a walnut-sized knob of butter and heat it until it is foaming (not brown). Pour in the beaten eggs and use a wooden spoon to stir the mixture and draw it away from the sides of the pan as it sets. Cook until the mixture has set and the underside is golden-brown. If making a filled omelette, add the filling now, spreading it over the whole surface. Fold one third of the omelette over the centre, then fold the other side over that. Turn out onto a hot plate and serve immediately.

SCRAMBLED EGGS (per person)

2 eggs

salt

black pepper

butter for cooking

Break the eggs into a mixing bowl, season them and beat them. In a non-stick pan, melt the butter, then pour the egg mixture into the pan. Cook over a low heat, stirring to bring the cooked egg away from the bottom and sides of the pan. Continue until all the egg has set, but turn it out onto a plate or serving dish while it looks as though it isn't fully cooked. It will continue to cook from its own heat, and will be over-done if you leave it in the pan until you think it is fully cooked.

FENNEL

TO BUY

Do not confuse the vegetable fennel with the herb fennel. The vegetable has swollen white stems which can be cooked or eaten raw.

TO STORE

Fennel can be kept for 4 - 5 days in the fridge.

TO PREPARE

Remove the tough outer layers before cutting the heart into halves or quarters, leaving some of the root end attached to each piece. For salads, and some cooked dishes, slice each portion thinly. You may need to remove tough portions of the core.

TO COOK

Fennel hearts can be braised in the same way as celery. Sliced, they can be lightly fried in butter to accompany chicken or fish.

FISH

TO BUY

Fish should feel firm and moist, and whole fish should have clear eyes.
The scales should glisten.

TO CLEAN AND PREPARE

Fish is normally gutted by the fishmonger, who should also do any
skinning and filleting that you require. You then need do no more than
rinse it under cold water.

Whole fish look better if the fins are removed and the tail is cut into a
neat V shape. Use kitchen scissors for both jobs. Large fish can then be
slashed two or three times on each side with a chef's knife, and slices of
lemon and/or herbs can be inserted into the cuts before cooking.

Fillets or 'steaks' should be checked for small bones by running your
fingers lightly over the flesh. Remove any bones with tweezers. Then
trim any ragged pieces of flesh or skin with a sharp knife before cooking.

TO STORE

Fresh fish can be stored in the fridge for up to 24 hours, but should be
well wrapped if the smell is not to taint other fridge contents.

TO COOK

Fish can be shallow or deep-fried. Although you can re-use the oil, keep
it in a separate jar marked 'fish'. Fish can also be grilled, barbecued,
baked, steamed or poached.

FISH AND CHIPS (For 4 People)

4 fillets of cod, haddock or plaice	75 g (3 oz) fine breadcrumbs or
1 tablespoon plain flour	150 ml (5 fl oz) batter (see page 34)
salt and white pepper	Oil or fat for frying
1 egg, beaten	1 kg (2 lbs) chips (see page 59)

Rinse the fish fillets and dry them on kitchen paper. Mix the flour, salt
and pepper, and spread this mixture on a flat plate or sheet of greaseproof
paper. Pour the beaten egg into another flat plate, and the breadcrumbs
on another. Dust each fillet with flour, then dip it first into the egg, then
the breadcrumbs, pressing them onto the fish if necessary. Lay them aside
until the chips are cooked. If using batter, dust the fillets with flour then
dip them into the batter immediately before putting them into the hot fat.
Cook the chips first, and put them in a covered dish in a warm oven to
keep hot while you cook the fish in a deep-fat fryer or a frying pan. If
you only have a small fryer, cook each fillet separately, adding it to the
chips to keep warm while you cook the rest. In a deep-fat fryer, each fillet

should take 6 - 8 minutes to cook or 3 - 4 minutes each side in a frying pan in shallow fat. Serve the fish and chips with wedges of lemon.

FISH CAKES

This is a good way to use up any left-over fish, but the potatoes should be freshly cooked and mashed.

225 g (8 oz) cooked fish or
  tinned salmon
225 g (8 oz) mashed potatoes
1 tablespoon milk
2 tablespoons chopped parsley
  (optional)

salt and pepper
1 egg, beaten
75 g (3 oz) breadcrumbs
oil for frying

Shred the flesh of the fish, making sure there are no bones in it. Mix it into the mashed potato with the milk and parsley. Season to your taste before forming the mixture into little cakes. Pour the egg into a plate and the breadcrumbs into another, dip the cakes into the egg then the breadcrumbs before shallow frying them until they are golden brown on each side, 3 - 4 minutes per side. Drain them on kitchen paper before serving.

FISH EGGS AND ROE

TO BUY

The most famous, and by far the most expensive, of fish eggs is caviare. It can be pink or black, depending on the type of sturgeon it came from, and the size of the individual eggs also varies. An alternative is lump fish roe, which can also be black or red, and which is vastly cheaper. Both are sold in small pots, and have been salted.   The other end of the scale is roe - from cod, grey mullet, or other fish. Cods roe can be soft (from the male fish) or hard (from the female), and may be sold cooked or smoked and in its natural state in a membrane, or in tins.

TO STORE

Caviare and roe should be kept in the fridge, and consumed within 3 days of purchase. Lump fish roe does not have to be kept in the fridge, and should be eaten within 1 month.

TO PREPARE

Caviare and lump fish roe need no preparation, but can be served straight from the pot. Both are served on toast, canapés, or on buckwheat pancakes called blinis, with sour cream.

Roe bought in its membrane should be soaked in cold water for 2 hours, then rinsed and drained before peeling off the membrane and mashing the contents.

TARAMASALATA

This is a creamy paste, served as a dip or spread, as a starter.

225 g (8 oz) soft cods roe
   or grey mullet roe
300 ml (10 fl oz) olive oil
60 ml (2 fl oz) boiling water

1 - 2 cloves garlic, crushed
squeeze of lemon juice
1 tablespoon finely chopped parsley

Prepare the roe as above and put it in a mixing bowl. Using an electric mixer, beat in the oil, a little at a time. When the mixture becomes hard and lumpy, stop adding oil and add boiling water, a little at a time, until the mixture has turned to a creamy texture. Now stir in the garlic and lemon juice, then turn the mixture into a serving bowl and sprinkle the parsley over the top. Cover the bowl with cling film and put it in the fridge for the flavours to develop – from 3 - 24 hours.

FLOUR

TO BUY

There are a number of types of flour:

- Plain flour, which is used for pastry and can be used for cakes if you add baking powder or bicarbonate of soda
- Self-raising flour, which has had raising agents added to it, and which is used for cakes
- Strong flour, which is made from hard types of wheat, and is used for bread-making and other recipes using yeast
- Pasta flour, which is used for making pasta and bread-making. The type marked 'grade 00' is the best.

All of these flours come in white or brown versions, the brown being further divided into 'wholewheat', which means just what it says – it is made from the whole grain, and 'wheatmeal' which has had the bran partially removed.

For most purposes, you will need only plain and self-raising flour. If you are short of space, keep plain flour and a small pot of baking powder.

TO STORE

All flour should be kept in a cool dry place, or in a sealed jar to keep out moisture. Wholewheat flour can be kept for 6 weeks, other flour for 3 months.

FRUIT SALADS

TO BUY

Fruit salads need to stand in their mixed form for several hours for the flavours to develop, so use fruit which is at its peak but not over the top, as the latter will start to ferment and spoil the salad. Crisp apples, strawberries, kiwi fruit, figs, grapes, melons, peaches or nectarines, orange, and banana are all acceptable. Some tinned fruit can be added in small quantities, such as lychees or mandarine oranges. Pineapple, whether fresh or tinned, is not a good idea, as it contains enzymes which can react badly with other fruits.

The trick in composing a good fruit salad is to choose fruit which offer a range of different levels of sweetness or sharpness, and also have a pleasing range of colours. So you might choose nectarines (slightly sharp, orange flesh with red skin), honeydew melon (very sweet, almost white flesh), strawberries (fruity flavour, red flesh and skin) and Granny Smith apples (tart flavour, white flesh and green skin). Or you could choose three types of melon (Honeydew, Charentais and Watermelon) for their three different colours, textures and tastes.

TO PREPARE

Simply cut the fruit into bite-sized pieces and put it all in a serving dish, then make sure it is covered with liquid. This liquid could be its own juice, added fruit juice, or a sweet white wine. You may feel the need to add a little sugar as well. Finally chill the salad for at least 2 hours.

Some fruit, such as apples and bananas, should be added at the last moment, as otherwise it will discolour.

GAME

Game is a term used for wild animals used as meat, and includes birds such as pheasants, small animals such as hares, and large animals such as deer or wild boar.

TO BUY

Game is now available from good supermarkets, dressed ready for cooking. It can also be bought from some specialist butchers or game dealers. If you buy it from the latter, ask them to draw (gut) it and pluck or skin it for you.

TO STORE

Once prepared, game should be kept in the fridge for up to 48 hours before cooking.

TO COOK

Cooking methods depend on the type of game, and also on its age. Young birds can be roasted but older birds may be tough and should be cooked slowly with liquid – either braised or casseroled. Hare is usually stewed or braised. Venison and boar, depending on the cut, should be cooked as you would the equivalent cut of beef or pork.

GARLIC

TO BUY

Garlic is sold as individual 'heads' which separate into many 'cloves'. Unless you are fond of garlic, it is best to buy it one head at a time. A good head of garlic will have at least 6 good-sized cloves on the outside, and at least as many small cloves further in. You should be able to feel how many big cloves there are. The whole thing should feel heavy and the cloves should feel solid. Reject garlic which feels light, where the covering skin is dry, or where you can see green shoots.

Most garlic is white, but you can sometimes buy violet coloured garlic, which has a better flavour. Freshly dug garlic is available in early summer. 'Elephant' garlic is a very large, mild tasting variety.

For those who do not like the smell of fresh garlic on their hands, you can also buy garlic purée in jars or squeeze tubes. Garlic powder is a poor substitute, and tends to set to a solid cake in the jar.

TO STORE

Store garlic in a cool dry place (not the refrigerator), away from other items such as eggs or bread, which might pick up its smell.

TO PREPARE

Separate as many cloves as you need from the head. Put each clove on a non-porous chopping board and use the blade of a heavy knife to press down on it to loosen the skin. Remove the skin and a thin slice from the base. If there is a green tip showing, slit the clove open and remove this, as it is bitter. Then crush the clove with a garlic crusher, or the blade of the knife. Alternatively, sprinkle it with coarse salt and chop it finely.

TO COOK

Many recipes tell you to start by frying garlic in oil or butter before adding other ingredients. This should be done over a gentle heat, as garlic burns easily and then becomes bitter, tainting the oil.

GARLIC BREAD

2 - 3 cloves of garlic
50 g (2 oz) butter, softened
1 French loaf

Preheat the oven to 180°C/ 350°F/ Gas Mark 4. Crush the garlic cloves and mix them into the butter. Cut diagonal slices almost through the loaf and spread the garlic butter inside the cuts. Wrap the bread in kitchen foil and put it in the oven for 10 - 12 minutes, to heat right through and melt the butter before serving.

GARNISHES

Garnishes do not necessarily add to the nutritional value of food, but they do make it look more inviting. Never forget that serving food is as much about visual appeal as about taste and aroma.

For savoury dishes, you can:
- sprinkle some chopped fresh herbs
- add a sprig or two of watercress or mint, or a little bunch of salad cress
- make spring onion or radish 'flowers' by slicing down one end several times, then dropping the onion or radish into iced water to make the cut ends curl back, cut a slice of cucumber from the edge to the centre, then twist the edges
- make decorative slices of cucumber, carrots or courgettes by dragging a fork down the skin before slicing
- cut a tomato in half then remove tiny wedges to create a crown effect, or make a butterfly – cut two wedges of tomato, then slice down inside the skin halfway and turn the flap back. Lay the wedges back to back on the plate and add two chives for antenna
- for fish dishes, make little fish from scraps of pastry
- garnish plain sauces with tiny dice of carrots, peppers or onion, make 'flowers' with carrot, cucumber skin and chives – peel the carrot and cut 4 grooves down the length before cutting slices for the flower, adding a chive for the stem and elongated diamonds of cucumber skin for leaves
- make lemon pigs – choose a lemon with a pronounced 'nose'. Make two holes above this with a toothpick and insert a clove in each for eyes. Cut a wedge out below the nose for a mouth. Cut and push up

2 triangles for the ears. Cut a thin strip of skin from the belly, tie a knot in it and make a hole with a toothpick then insert the strip for a tail. Finally, break 2 toothpicks in half and use them for legs.

For sweet dishes, you can:
- sift a little icing sugar and/or cocoa powder over the surface of cakes or buns, or create a pattern on a cake by laying a paper doily over it before sifting icing sugar, then carefully remove the doily to leave the pattern
- sprinkle chopped toasted nuts
- lay a small sprig of mint or a string of red currants on the dish
- make chocolate curls by using a vegetable peeler on the edge of a chocolate bar
- make chocolate boxes with square after-dinner mints, stuck together with a filling of whipped cream and topped with a fan-cut strawberry
- make some coloured sugar for sprinkling – add 1 drop of food colouring to a small jar of granulated sugar, stir and shake until the colour has spread through all the sugar.

GLOBE ARTICHOKES

TO BUY
Globe artichokes are related to thistles, and what you eat is the flower-head, before it opens. The whole head should be heavy and shiny, and the fleshy leaf-like bracts should be no more than slightly open. Reject specimens which are turning brown and shrivelled. You can also buy tinned artichoke hearts, but they are expensive and pretty tasteless, so there is little point.

TO STORE
Globe artichokes should be cooked within 2 days of purchase, and eaten within another day. They should be kept at room temperature until cooked, then in a fridge.

TO PREPARE AND COOK
Artichokes discolour when cut, so start by preparing a large saucepan of acidulated water. Other than trimming the base level, you do not have to do any more, but some people like to snip off the sharp tips of the bracts. Drop each one into the water as you finish it. Salt the water and bring it to the boil, then cover the pan and simmer for 15 - 20 minutes, depending on how big the artichokes are. Test them for doneness by tweaking a bract – if it comes away in your hand, they are done and can be drained, upside-down. If you want to serve them with a filling, you need to remove the inedible 'choke' in the centre. Spread the bracts with your fingers, working your way inwards until you reach the fine strands in the

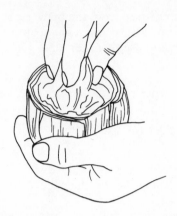 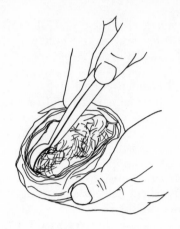

middle. Pull these out and discard them, then use a teaspoon to scrape out any residue, leaving the heart underneath.

Fillings include baby peas in sour cream, breadcrumbs with finely chopped bacon and onion, or ricotta cheese with hard-boiled egg and a Parmesan topping. After filling, put the artichokes in a single layer in a baking dish, drizzle a little olive oil over them, and bake at 160°C/325°F/ Gas Mark 3 for 50 - 60 minutes.

GOOSEBERRIES

TO BUY
Pink gooseberries are sweet enough to eat raw. Green berries are sharp-tasting and need to be cooked with sugar.

TO STORE
Fresh gooseberries can be kept in a cool dry place for up to 48 hours, or frozen for up to 12 months.

TO PREPARE
Fresh gooseberries should be 'topped and tailed'. This means snipping off the stem and remains of the flower, then they should be rinsed before cooking.

TO COOK
Put the berries in a saucepan with sugar and 2 tablespoons water. For 450 g (1 lb) berries you will need about 100 g (4 oz) sugar, depending on your taste. Cover the pan and put it to cook over medium heat for 20 - 25 minutes, checking at intervals that there is sufficient liquid. Once they have softened, they will make their own liquid. You may not need all this liquid, in which case strain the berries through a sieve.

GOOSEBERRY FOOL

450 g (1 lb) gooseberries
100 g (4 oz) sugar
150 ml (5 fl oz) custard
  (see page 66)

150 ml (5 fl oz) double cream
caster sugar for serving

Cook the berries and sugar as above, then strain them to remove excess
liquid before using a fork to break them down to pulp. Let them cool
completely, then chill in the fridge for 2 - 3 hours. Make the custard, cool
it and chill it. Whip the cream to the soft peaks stage.

Turn the gooseberries into a large bowl and gently fold in the custard,
then the cream. Spoon the mixture into 4 dishes (traditionally long-
stemmed glasses) and chill for a further 2 hours before serving. Offer
caster sugar for diners who have a sweeter tooth than you!

GRAINS

TO BUY

There are many different types of edible grain, from the familiar rice
(see page 133) to the nutritious but uncommon quinoa. Some of them are
available in most supermarkets, others from health food stores.

BARLEY
Barley is usually sold as 'pearl' barley – small polished grains which can
be used to make lemon barley water (see page 92), added to lamb stews,
or cooked on their own and used like rice as a base for savoury dishes.
Health food stores also stock barley flakes, which look like rolled oats
and can be used in muesli.

BUCKWHEAT
Sometimes known as Kasha, buckwheat isn't strictly speaking a grain, but
a small triangular seed of a plant related to rhubarb. It is usually dry-
roasted in a saucepan for 4 - 5 minutes before butter or oil is added to
briefly fry it, then water is added to simmer it for 10 - 15 minutes. It can
be served on its own, or cooked with other vegetables such as lentils and
onions. It is also ground into flour, which is used to make blinis (small
pancakes served with sour cream and caviare) or Breton pancakes.

CORN
Here, corn means maize, rather than the cereals (barley, oats, rye and
wheat) which are sometimes called corn in the UK. It is normally used in
its ground form of cornmeal, also known as polenta. Polenta is
traditionally cooked by pouring a stream of meal into a pan of boiling
water, then stirring continuously for the 30 or more minutes it takes to

cook. Now you can buy 'instant' polenta which cooks in minutes. Once cooked, it has the texture of mashed potatoes and you can either serve it straightaway, with a meat or mushroom stew, or leave it to cool, when it sets, then slice it and fry or bake slices to serve with stews or cheese dishes.

COUSCOUS
Couscous is made from wheat, and is cooked by being steamed over a stew of meat and/or vegetables. You can now get quick couscous which only needs to be soaked in boiling water for a few minutes.

MILLET
Millet is a very small grain which can be substituted for rice in milk puddings or risottos. Keep an eye on it while it cooks, as it absorbs a lot of water and can boil dry and burn. You can also get millet flour to add to wheat flour for bread making. You will probably have to go to a health food store for it.

OATS
Oats are usually sold as flakes, either the readily available porridge oats, or larger toasted flakes for bread making and muesli.

QUINOA
Quinoa is another non-cereal grain, sometimes sold as 'keen-wa' (which is how you pronounce its name). You will probably have to go to a health food store for it. It is highly nutritious and can be eaten by people with gluten allergies. Cook it like rice, and use it as a rice-substitute, in sweet or savoury dishes.

RYE
Rye is normally sold ground into flour for bread-making, but it can also be bought as flakes from health food shops.

WHEAT
Wheat is sold in health food stores as whole grains, sometimes called wheat berries, which can be cooked like rice, although they take longer to cook. They make an excellent salad, or you can buy bulgar wheat which has been steamed and roasted. Served with chopped mint and lemon juice, this is known as Tabbouleh. You can also get wholewheat flakes which can be used in muesli.

WILD RICE
Not rice at all, but a grain which looks like dark grey rice grains. It is difficult to harvest and therefore expensive, but has a nutty taste and is often mixed with rice for savoury dishes.

TO STORE

All grains or ground meals should be stored in airtight containers at room temperature. Once the packet is open, it is best to use them within 6 weeks.

HOME-MADE MUESLI

The basis of muesli is traditionally oat flakes, sultanas and flaked nuts, but you can add anything else you like to it from the list below. Make up big batches of it and keep them in an airtight container. Aim for proportions of roughly twice as much flaked grain as dried fruit and half as much nuts to dried fruit.

Serve it with milk, which can be full-cream or skimmed, according to your own taste. If you like it sweet, add honey when serving rather than sugar. You can also add fresh fruit when serving it, such as slices of apple, banana, peach, strawberry or plum.

The flaked grains could be barley, oats, rye or wheat. The dried fruit could be currants, raisins, sultanas, chopped dates, dried banana, apple, apricot, or fig. The nuts could be peanuts, almonds, hazel, walnuts, pecans. The other seeds could be sunflower seeds, pumpkin seeds etc.

GRAVY

TO PREPARE

To make real gravy, you need the juices from the meat that have collected in the roasting tin, and some hot liquid. This could be the water in which you have cooked the vegetables, or homemade stock. If all else fails, use a stock cube to make up stock. You will also need 1 tablespoon plain flour.

When the meat is cooked, take it from the roasting tin and put it on a carving dish and keep it somewhere warm to rest for 15 - 30 minutes. Pour the fat and liquid from the tin into a gravy separator or tall bowl. Let it stand for a minute or so to separate, then pour all but 1 - 2 tablespoons of the fat into another bowl before pouring the rest of the fat back into the roasting tin. Put the tin over a low heat and stir in first the flour and then the rest of the roasting liquid. Let it cook for a couple of minutes while you strain the vegetables, then add the vegetable water or stock, 2 tablespoons at a time, stirring each lot in before adding more until you have the thickness you want. Taste and add salt if necessary. Turn the heat up and let the gravy cook for 4 - 5 minutes before pouring it into a warm jug or gravy boat.

HERBS

TO BUY
Fresh herbs are now available all year in big supermarkets, either growing in pots, or packed in small trays. Dried herbs are useful to keep in the store cupboard, but in many cases do not retain their flavour. Thyme, sage, rosemary, bay leaves and oregano are good dried; basil, tarragon, mint, chives and parsley are not.

TO CLEAN
Fresh herbs need no more than gentle rinsing under a cold tap, then shaking dry.

TO STORE
Dried herbs should be kept in airtight jars, for up to 6 months. Chopped fresh herbs can be frozen in a little water in ice-cube trays, or stored in olive oil in a sealed jar.

TO PREPARE FRESH HERBS
Mint, basil, sage and parsley can be chopped with a sharp knife. Thyme and chives are easily snipped with sharp kitchen scissors.

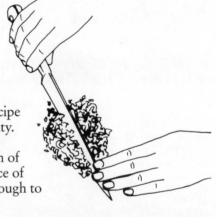

TO COOK
If you have only dried herbs when a recipe calls for fresh, use half the stated quantity. To make a bouquet garni, make a little bunch of 1 bay leaf, and 2 -3 sprigs each of thyme and parsley. Tie them with a piece of kitchen string, leaving the ends long enough to attach to the handle of the pan.

JAM

TO BUY
Jam comes in two basic types - 'standard' jam, which must contain a minimum of 35% fruit, and 'extra' jam (which may also be called 'preserve'), which must have a minimum of 45% fruit. The best jams contain only fruit, sugar, and perhaps a little citric acid and some pectin. Other jams may contain various 'preservatives'. For eating as a spread on bread or toast, choose whichever flavour of jam suits your taste. As an ingredient in cakes and puddings, the most useful jams are apricot, raspberry and strawberry.

TO STORE

Once opened, most jams should be kept in the fridge.

TO MAKE JAM

For all jams, you need fruit which is perfectly ripe but not over-ripe. Blemished fruit is usually past its best, and will not make good jam. Some fruits such as cherries, strawberries and rhubarb, do not jellify properly on their own, and you may need to add some pectin to aid setting. Most jam consists of equal weight of fruit and sugar, but the exact quantities vary from recipe to recipe.

A wide preserving pan is the classic cooking pan, but you can make jam in a large saucepan without a lid. The principle of jam-making is boiling which evaporates the water content of the fruit juice, thickening the mixture, thus encouraging it to set. (You can also make small quantities of jam in the microwave.) Test for the setting point by putting a spoonful of jam on a cold saucer and putting it in the fridge for a few minutes. Then push the edge of the jam with a finger – if the surface wrinkles, the jam is ready and can be bottled.

While the jam is cooking, sterilise the jars (see page 11). When the jam is ready to bottle, first fill the jars with very hot water to warm them, then empty this out and fill the jars. Jam with large pieces of whole fruit should be allowed to cool slightly before bottling, as this stops the pieces rising to the top as it cools. Otherwise fill the jars straightaway. Let the full jars cool completely before putting the lids on.

STRAWBERRY JAM (makes 1 ½ kg (3 lbs) jam)

1 kg (2 lbs) ripe but dry
   strawberries

700 g (1 ½ lbs) sugar
juice of 1 lemon

Remove the hulls (leafy top) from the strawberries. If you want whole berries in the jam, put them in a big pan, spread the sugar and lemon juice over them and leave them for 8 - 10 hours. Otherwise, quarter the berries and put them in the pan with the sugar and lemon juice. Put the pan over a very low heat, stirring very gently at brief intervals until the sugar has dissolved and the juice is coming out of the berries. Then turn up the heat and cook for 10 minutes, stirring frequently. Draw the pan off the heat and test for setting.

JELLY

TO BUY

Packet jellies are available in many flavours, but be sure to check the contents list as many are fruit 'flavoured' rather than the real thing.

However, if these are all that is available, you can improve them by using fruit juice instead of water when you make them up. Note that jellies made with gelatine are not suitable for vegetarians, in which case use agar-agar.

TO STORE

Made jellies can be kept in the fridge for up to 24 hours.
You can make your own jellies from fruit juice and gelatine.

450 g (1 lb) fresh fruit (pineapple is not suitable as it contains enzymes which impede setting) 100 g (4 oz) caster sugar	juice of 1 lemon 300 ml (10 fl oz) water 2 sachets of gelatine (or equivalent – sachets contain 11 g [0.4 oz] each)

Liquidise the fruit, sugar, lemon juice and water together and strain the resulting purée through a fine sieve. Check for sweetness and add more sugar if necessary. Dissolve the gelatine in a few tablespoons warm water, then stir it into the fruit purée. Pour the jelly into one large or up to 6 small dishes and chill for 3 - 4 hours until set.

JERUSALEM ARTICHOKES

TO BUY

Jerusalem artichokes are a tuber, and no relation to globe artichokes. They look like a small potato, but have flesh which is crisp and crunchy when raw, and slightly watery when cooked. They can cause severe flatulence in some people, so only serve a few until you find out how your family react to them. They should be firm and heavy. Reject specimens which are shrivelled and feel flabby. Choose the least knobbly ones, as these are easier to peel.

TO STORE

Jerusalem artichokes should be kept in a very cool place, as they soon shrivel at room temperature. Try to use them within a week of purchase.

TO PREPARE

Jerusalem artichokes discolour when peeled, so drop them into acidulated water as you finish each one. The skin is very thin, so peel them thinly.

TO COOK

Jerusalem artichokes can be served raw in salads. Otherwise cook them in any of the ways you cook potatoes - boiled, roast, fried, steamed, mashed, or in soup. As the flesh is delicate, they need only about two-thirds of the cooking time of a potato.

KEBABS

Kebabs are small pieces of meat, vegetable, cheese or fruit, arranged on skewers and cooked under a grill or on a barbecue.

TO PREPARE

Wooden skewers should be soaked in water for an hour before threading the ingredients onto them. Whether wooden or metal, skewers should be flat, to prevent the food slipping when you turn it.

To ensure that they cook evenly, cut all ingredients to the same size. Ingredients may be marinated before being threaded onto the skewers, or can be painted with flavoured oil or marinade during cooking.

TO COOK

After threading the ingredients on the skewers, alternating colours and flavours attractively on each skewer, preheat the grill for about 5 minutes at its highest setting, then turn it down to medium heat before putting the skewers of food to cook. They will need a total of 10 - 12 minutes cooking, and should be turned two or three times.

VEGETABLE KEBABS

2 large peppers, 1 red and 1 green,
   cut into pieces approximately
   2cm (1") square
8 cherry tomatoes
8 button mushrooms
2 small courgettes,
   cut into chunks

8 small onions
225 g (8 oz) mozarella cheese,
   (or tofu) cubed
8 tablespoons olive oil
1 tablespoon white wine vinegar
1 tablespoon chopped
   fresh herbs

Mix all the ingredients together in a large bowl, then cover the bowl and leave to marinate for at least 2 hours before threading onto skewers and cooking.

CHICKEN KEBABS

Proceed as for vegetable kebabs, substituting chicken breast for the mozarella cheese.

MEAT KEBABS

Proceed as above, substituting beef, lamb or pork for the chicken, and red wine vinegar for the white wine vinegar. Control the degree of cooking of the meat by the spacing on the skewer – well separated for well-done, closer for less well-done.

FRUIT KEBABS

Choose a selection of fruit which is solid enough to put on skewers -

apple, banana, firm peaches or nectarines, sections of orange, pineapple or grapes. Add marshmallows if desired. Drizzle with a little thin honey before cooking.

KIPPERS AND OTHER SMOKED FISH

TO BUY
There is such a wide range of smoked fish products that what you buy is very much a matter of individual taste. Choose from:
- kippers, either loose or prepacked, the latter often in handy 'boil in the bag' packs which prevent the smell of cooking from permeating the whole house.
- bloaters, usually sold loose.
- smoked salmon (see page 136)
- other smoked fish, such as trout, mackerel, haddock, or eel.

TO STORE
Loose kippers and bloaters should, theoretically, keep indefinitely hung up in a larder, as they have been dried and smoked precisely to make them keep. They do have a distinctive odour, though, so most people are unlikely to buy more than they need immediately. Ready-to-cook packs, whether vacuum packed or frozen, will have a 'use by' date which you should follow.

Other smoked fish should be used within 48 hours of purchase.

TO PREPARE
Bloaters are cured with their guts in to give them their distinctive flavour, so before cooking them, you have to split them and remove the guts. Other smoked fish needs no special preparation, except that haddock should be rinsed.

TO COOK
Kippers and bloaters can be fried or grilled. They can be made into pâté once cooked.

Finnan haddock and Arbroath smokies are usually cooked in the oven with a little milk or butter. Haddock fillets are usually poached in water or milk – place the fillets in a single layer in a large saucepan and cover them with milk or a mixture of milk and water, bring the liquid to the boil then turn it down to simmer gently for 5 minutes. (For a filling breakfast or brunch, serve these poached fillets with a poached egg on top.)

Smoked salmon, trout and eel are usually served as they are, but can be made into soufflés.

KIWI FRUIT

TO BUY

Kiwi fruit are ready to eat when they give slightly when gently pressed. They are a good source of Vitamin C, and can be used to make jam as well as attractive slices for fruit salads and cakes.

TO PREPARE

With a sharp pointed knife, cut out the hard part at each end, then use a vegetable peeler to remove the skin. Then cut thin slices across the width of the fruit for the most attractive result. They can also be cut in half and eaten with a spoon, like a boiled egg.

LAMB

TO BUY

To roast, choose leg or shoulder. To grill or fry, choose chops, cutlets, lamb fillet or leg steaks. For stews and casseroles, choose best end of neck.

TO STORE

All raw meat should be stored in a refrigerator, for up to 48 hours. Lamb can be frozen, but should be tightly wrapped to prevent freezer 'burn'. Freeze joints and steaks for up to 12 months, slices and cubes for up to 8 months, mince for up to 3 months.

TO PREPARE

Roasting joints and leg steaks may need a little trimming to remove excess fat. Snip through the edging fat on steaks with kitchen scissors at 2 cm (1") intervals to prevent them curling up during cooking. Otherwise, just rinse the meat under cold water and dry with kitchen paper before cooking.

TO COOK

Chops, cutlets and other small cuts of lamb may be fried or grilled. For cooking times, see steaks on page 38.

Joints of lamb (legs, shoulders, or rolled and stuffed breast) should be cooked at 230°C/450°F/ Gas Mark 8 for 30 minutes, then the heat should be turned down to 180°C/350°F/ Gas Mark 4 for a further 60 minutes per kilo (30 minutes per lb).

Although lamb fat is alright for making gravy, it is not suitable to be saved for other purposes.

LEAFY SALADS

Salad leaves used to mean soft green (or iceberg) lettuce, but now you can buy a wide variety of salad leaves as well as many types of lettuce. Endive and chicory (the red-leaved version is called radicchio) are slightly bitter, as is blanched dandelion. Rocket is peppery. Lambs lettuce is very bland, as are the various Chinese leaves. Spinach is slightly sharp tasting. Watercress is quite hot. Some mixtures include herbs, thinly shredded red or white cabbage, and young beetroot leaves.

TO BUY

Whole heads of lettuce or other salad leaves will keep for several days, but ready prepared salads deteriorate quickly, so buy the latter in small quantities.

TO STORE

All types of whole unwashed salad leaves can be kept in the fridge for 3 - 4 days. Check the packet for keeping times on ready-prepared leaves.

TO CLEAN

All salad leaves should be washed thoroughly just before serving. Dunk them in a large bowl of cold water under a running tap, then dry them. If you do not have a salad spinner, take handfuls of leaves and shake them to remove most of the water, then put them in a clean tea-towel, gather up the corners and shake thoroughly. Turn the leaves onto another towel and pat off any remaining water.

TO PREPARE

Large leaves should be torn into smaller pieces. Add salad dressings at the last minute and only dress as much as will be eaten straightaway, as dressings make the leaves wilt after a couple of hours. Ideally, pass dressings separately for each diner to add their own. For the recipe for vinaigrette dressing, see page 154.

LEEKS

TO BUY

Leeks are at their best during the winter months. As spring progresses, they start to flower, and may contain a woody core. Choose fat, heavy specimens with more white than green. Reject any which are turning yellow.

TO STORE

Leeks should be kept in a cool dry place for up to 1 week after buying.

TO CLEAN AND PREPARE

Leeks need to be thoroughly washed to remove any soil which may have fallen between the leaves. Start by cutting off the roots and removing any coarse outer leaves and the coarse top. Cut off the white part, which should not need washing, and slice it into rounds. Then cut the green part in half lengthways and rinse it thoroughly under running cold water before slicing it as before.

TO COOK

Leeks can be added to stews or casseroles, used to make soup (see page 142), or cooked on their own. They tend to become water-logged if boiled, so it is best to steam them or cook them in the microwave in a plastic bag or covered dish, with only a sprinkling of water.

LEMONS

TO BUY

The juiciest lemons are those which have a smooth skin and feel heavy. Unless they are marked 'unwaxed' or 'organic', they will have a thin coat of protective wax. When you want to use the zest or the skin, either choose unwaxed organic fruit or wash it well in warm water before use.

TO CLEAN

Regardless of waxed or unwaxed skin, wash or wipe lemons before use.

TO STORE

Whole lemons can be kept at room temperature for many weeks, but you should check at intervals that they are not drying out or starting to rot. Lemons whose skins have become dry and hard may still contain usable juice. Lemons can be frozen whole or as juice, for up to 12 months.

TO PREPARE

To extract the juice from a lemon, cut it in half through its 'equator' and remove the biggest pips. Then either press each half down onto a domed squeezer and rotate a few times, or hold the half in one hand over a bowl and push the tines of a fork into it, rotate them and squeeze. Always strain to remove the pips before using the juice.

To prepare sections for diners to squeeze on their food, either serve half lemons, cut as above, or cut each lemon into wedges lengthways. Round slices are a nuisance to handle.

LEMON BARLEY WATER

100 g (4 oz) granulated sugar
zest and juice of 3 large lemons

3 tablespoons pearl barley
1 litre (2 pts) water

Put the sugar, lemon zest and juice in a bowl. Put the barley and water in a saucepan, bring to the boil and simmer for 10 - 15 minutes. Turn off the heat, then add the sugar and lemon mixture to the pan. Stir and leave it to cool. Strain into a jug and chill before serving.

LENTILS

TO BUY
Choose red lentils for soups or dhal, green, brown, or Puy lentils for salads.

TO CLEAN
It is wise to check that packets of lentils do not include small stones. Rinse them just before cooking.

TO STORE
Store, in the packet, in a dry cupboard. Once the packet is open, keep the unused lentils in a sealed box or jar. Lentils keep a long time but start to deteriorate after 6 months. Leftover cooked lentils can be kept in the fridge in a plastic bag or sealed dish for 24 hours.

TO COOK
For 4 people, you will need 225 g (8 oz) lentils, and 600 ml (1 pint) water. Lentils do not need soaking. Rinse them and put them in a saucepan with the water. Do not add salt until the end of the cooking time. Bring the water to the boil, then turn the heat down to simmer for 20 - 30 minutes. All the water should have been absorbed and the lentils should be tender but not mushy.

DHAL

1 tablespoon ghee or vegetable oil
2 cloves garlic, crushed
1 teaspoon ground ginger
1 teaspoon ground turmeric
1 tablespoon white wine vinegar

225 g (8 oz) red or yellow lentils
600 ml (1 pt) water
1 teaspoon salt
chopped fresh coriander to garnish

In a saucepan, heat the oil and fry the garlic, ground ginger and turmeric for a few moments, then stir in the vinegar to make a paste. Add the lentils and stir briefly, then add the water. Bring to the boil, then simmer for 20 - 30 minutes until the lentils are soft and most of the liquid has been absorbed. Add salt and remove the pan from the heat and use a potato masher to mash the lentils, adding a little boiling water to loosen the mixture if necessary. Serve with the coriander sprinkled on top.

PUY LENTIL SALAD

225 g (8 oz) Puy lentils
600 ml (1 pt) water
3 small whole onions,
  each with a clove stuck in it
2 carrots, peeled and quartered
1 bayleaf
1 teaspoon salt

4 hard-boiled eggs,
  shelled and quartered
2 teaspoons Dijon-style mustard
2 tablespoons olive oil
black pepper
small bunch chives

Put the lentils, water, onions, carrots and bayleaf into a saucepan, bring to the boil, and simmer for 20 minutes until the lentils are soft. Drain, remove the onions, carrots and bayleaf, sprinkle with salt and leave to cool. Meanwhile, whisk the mustard into the oil and snip the chives. To serve, heap the lentils in a dish, pour the mustardy oil over them, grind the pepper over the top, arrange the eggs round the dish and sprinkle the chives on top.

LIVER

TO BUY

Calves' or lambs' liver is more expensive but less strong tasting than pigs' or ox liver. Buy ready cut slices from a supermarket, or ask your butcher to cut it for you. Chicken or duck livers are usually sold in tubs, fresh or frozen. Foie gras is liver from force-fed ducks or geese, and can be bought raw in vacuum packs, or cooked in pots or tins.

TO STORE

Raw liver, unless vacuum packed, should be used on the day it is purchased. Liver can be frozen for up to 3 months.

TO PREPARE

Raw livers often have tough internal tubes, which should be cut out with kitchen scissors. Whole livers from calves, lambs, ox or pigs are covered in a thin membrane which should be snipped and peeled away before slicing. Ox or pigs liver can be soaked in milk overnight to reduce the strong taste. (Throw the milk away.)

TO COOK

Liver should be cooked quickly, as prolonged cooking makes it tough. The best way to cook meat liver is to slice it thinly, sprinkle it with a light dusting of flour, and flash fry it in olive oil or butter for 2 - 3 minutes each side. Liver can also be braised with bacon, onions and tomatoes.

Chicken or duck livers should be fried whole, in butter, for 1 - 2 minutes each side.

MANGO

TO BUY

Mangoes can be bought fresh, tinned in slices or puréed, or as dried pieces. Tinned slices in syrup are pleasant enough, but a pale shadow of a ripe fresh mango. Tinned purée is better, but you may have to go to an Indian grocer for it. The best of the fresh mangoes are 'Alphonso', small golden curved fruit available in early spring. Fresh mangoes are ready to eat when they feel slightly soft and have an intense fruity scent. Reject specimens which look bruised or which have discoloured patches.

TO STORE

Fresh mangoes should be kept at room temperature. If kept in a fruit bowl, they should be kept on top to avoid bruising.

TO PREPARE

Ripe mangoes are very juicy, so deal with them over a bowl to catch drips, and near the sink so you can rinse your hands. (Serious mango eaters say the best way to eat them is in the bath!)

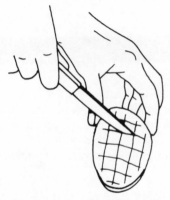

They have a large flat woody stone which has to be removed. Lay the fruit on a flat surface, and insert a sharp knife into one side, just above the middle line until you can feel the stone. Cut right through the fruit close to the stone to remove a thick slice. Turn it over and repeat, then slice any remaining flesh away from the sides of the stone. For slices, gently remove the skin with a vegetable peeler before slicing the flesh. Otherwise, holding one of the large pieces in one hand, skin side down, (ideally over a bowl to catch the juice) cut through the flesh to, but not through, the skin laterally, then horizontally to make squares. Then press the base of the piece upwards to make a 'hedgehog' before cutting the squares off the skin.

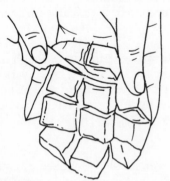

QUICK MANGO PARFAIT

1 x 400 g tin of mango purée
1 x 568 ml pot of double cream
　or pouring yoghurt
25 g (1 oz) flaked almonds
　or hazelnuts

toasted boudoir biscuits or
fan-shaped ice-cream wafers

Open the tin of mango and stir it. Pour the contents into 4 serving dishes, then carefully pour a layer of cream/yoghurt on top. Sprinkle the flaked nuts on to decorate. Refrigerate for about an hour. Just before serving, put 2 boudoir biscuits or 1 ice-cream fan wafer into each dish.

MARROW

TO BUY

Marrows have very little flavour and even that diminishes as they get bigger. So choose small specimens and reject any over 30 cm (12") long. They should feel heavy for their size, and the skin should be shiny and unblemished.

TO STORE

Marrows will keep for several weeks at room temperature, but should be checked over regularly for blemishes which indicate deterioration.

TO PREPARE

For all purposes, peel marrows, cut them open and remove all the seeds and stringy flesh which surrounds them. They can then be cut into chunks, or stuffed as thick rounds or halves.

TO COOK

Marrows have a watery flesh, so they should not be boiled as this will only make them more watery. To serve as an accompaniment, stew them in a lidded saucepan with sufficient butter to prevent their sticking, and served with plenty of chopped parsley and black pepper. Marrow for stuffing should either be steamed before stuffing, then baked, or wrapped tightly in foil after stuffing and baked slowly to release the juices.

MAYONNAISE

Home-made mayonnaise has a reputation for being difficult, but all it needs is a little patience. Once you have mastered basic mayonnaise, there are a number of simple variations that will allow you to prepare several well-known dishes.

TO PREPARE

2 egg yolks
½ level teaspoon salt
a few grinds of black pepper
a pinch of mustard powder

300 ml (10 fl oz) olive oil,
or a mixture of olive oil
and sunflower oil
1 tablespoon lemon juice

BY HAND
Put the egg yolks in a mixing bowl with the salt, pepper, and mustard.

95

With a hand or electric whisk, beat the yolks until they have thickened a little. Put the oil in a jug with a good lip for pouring, and drip it onto the yolks, beating them as you pour. The mixture should be smooth and shiny throughout the process. Keep pouring slowly and beating until you have used about half of the oil. Now beat in half of the lemon juice, then you can beat in the rest of the oil, pouring it a little faster. Finally, beat in the rest of the lemon juice, taste the mixture and add more salt or pepper as necessary.

If your mayonnaise curdles or separates, add 1 tablespoon hot water and beat vigorously. If this doesn't work, start again with fresh egg yolks and oil in a clean bowl, then when the new mixture has thickened, gradually beat the old mixture into it, adjusting the texture with more oil or lemon juice.

IN A BLENDER OR FOOD PROCESSOR
Put the egg yolks, salt, pepper and mustard powder in the machine and blend briefly to mix them. With the motor running, slowly add two-thirds of the oil, starting a few drips at a time. Add the lemon juice and blend it in, then the rest of the oil. Taste and adjust the seasoning as necessary.

TO STORE
Transfer the mayonnaise to a serving bowl, and if not using it immediately, press a piece of greaseproof paper onto the surface to prevent a skin forming. You can keep it in a refrigerator for up to two weeks in a sealed jar, but take it out of the fridge an hour before serving or it may separate when stirred.

VARIATIONS
For garlic mayonnaise, add 2 crushed cloves of garlic to the basic mixture with the salt and pepper.
For prawn cocktail sauce, add 2 level teaspoons tomato ketchup to the basic mixture at the end.
For curry mayonnaise to make coronation chicken, beat 2-3 teaspoons mild curry powder and 2 tablespoons mango chutney (remove any big lumps of mango) into the basic mixture at the end, then use this to coat 450 g (1 lb) cooked chicken.

MELON

TO BUY
Melons are ripe when the end away from the stalk gives a little and they smell sweet and fruity. Ogen or Charentais (round and orangey-pink) have pink flesh. Honeydew melons (oblong and yellow) have pale flesh

and are the sweetest. Both have all the pips in the middle, which can easily be scooped out with a spoon before serving. Watermelons (round with thick green skin) have watery bright pink flesh with hard black pips dotted through it.

TO STORE

Melons should be stored at room temperature until you are ready to prepare them, after which they can be chilled in the fridge. If not quite ripe when purchased, they will ripen best on a sunny windowsill.

TO PREPARE

Ogen or Charentais melons are traditionally served cut in half. Caster sugar can be sprinkled on them in the kitchen or by the diner, or sherry can be poured into the cavity which held the seeds.

Honeydew melons are traditionally served in slices cut lengthways, with the flesh separated from the rind. Caster sugar or ground ginger can be served with them, or a slice of orange can be attached to a toothpick to resemble a sail to make a melon 'boat'. They can also be served as a more substantial starter with a couple of very thin slices of Parma ham.

Watermelons are best served cut into chunks (after removing the seeds) and served in a dish.

All melons can have the flesh scooped out with a melon 'baller' which makes little balls, which can then be served on their own, or as part of a fruit cocktail.

MERINGUE

There are two types of meringue which can be easily made by the home cook – the soft sort which is used to top sweet pies, and the hard sort which is used for confectionery. Both are made from a basic mixture of egg white and sugar, which is then cooked very slowly. In both cases, the whipping bowl and utensils should be meticulously clean, and care should be taken when separating the eggs that no yolk gets into the white. The egg white should be at room temperature.

PIE-TOPPING MERINGUE

whites of 2 eggs
100g (4 oz) caster sugar

In a large bowl, whip the egg whites to the stiff peaks stage. Add a quarter of the sugar and beat it in, then repeat until all the sugar has been incorporated. Use a palette knife to spread the meringue over the top of your filled pie, spreading right to the outer edge of the pastry to seal the rim. Cook at 150°C/300°F/ Gas Mark 2 for 45 minutes, until the top is pale gold but the inside of the meringue is still soft.

CREAM-FILLED MERINGUES

whites of 2 eggs
3 - 4 drops vanilla essence
100 g (4 oz) caster sugar

150 ml (5 fl oz) double or
  whipping cream

Prepare the baking trays either by brushing them with olive oil or melted butter, or by lining them with greaseproof paper or non-stick silicone paper. Preheat the oven to 100°C/200°F/ Gas Mark ¼.

Whip the egg whites to the stiff peaks stage. Add the vanilla essence, then half the sugar and whisk it in slowly, then add the rest of the sugar and whisk it in. Using two tablespoons, scoop a spoonful of the mixture out of the bowl with one spoon, then use the other spoon to scoop it onto the baking tray. Continue with the rest of the mixture – it should be sufficient for 12 meringues. Alternatively, transfer the mixture to a piping bag fitted with a star nozzle and pipe out 12 shapes. Dust the shapes with a little extra sugar.

Bake the meringues for 2 - 3 hours, until they feel crisp on the outside. Remove them from the baking tray with a warmed palette knife, and leave to cool on a wire rack.

Whip the cream to the stiff peaks stage, and use it to sandwich the meringues together in pairs.

MINCE

TO BUY

Most people, when they say 'mince' mean beef, but you can now buy minced lamb, pork, turkey and chicken, all of which are useful for dishes such as shepherds pie, moussaka, burgers, home-made sausages, meat loaf or meat balls. In all cases, buy the best quality mince you can, as cheaper versions often contain a high proportion of fat, gristle, and other uninviting portions of animals such as udders. By the time you've got rid of the fat and nasty bits, you end up having paid the same amount that you would if you'd bought top quality.

Whichever type of meat you buy as mince, it should be pink, not going brown, and you should not be able to see too much white fat. If pre-packed, it should not be swimming in bloody liquid.

TO STORE

Minced meat should be kept in the fridge and used within 24 hours of purchase, unless frozen. Uncooked mince or prepared mince dishes such as burgers can be frozen for up to 3 months. Meat loaf can be kept in the freezer for up to 1 month.

TO PREPARE

Mince does not need any preparation before cooking. When mixing minced meat with other ingredients, many recipes suggest that you mix it with your hands. If you do not like the idea of handling mince, put it and the other ingredients in a large plastic bag, seal it and squidge the contents together through the plastic.

TO COOK

What puts many people off the idea of mince is memories of nasty grey stuff, swimming in fatty liquid – the result of dumping the raw mince in water and boiling it. To avoid this, and to speed up the cooking process, unless you are making burgers, sausages or stuffing, you should start by dry-frying the mince a little at a time, breaking up the lumps with a wooden spoon as it cooks, then drain off as much of the fat as possible before proceeding.

The recipe below is for an all-purpose savoury mince, which can be converted into many dishes with the addition of appropriate ingredients. If you have a freezer, it is worth making up batches of this recipe and freezing it in meal-sized containers.

ALL-PURPOSE SAVOURY MINCE

1 kilo (2 lbs) good quality
   minced meat
2 medium to large onions,
   finely chopped
2 stock cubes appropriate to the
   type of meat, made up to
   600 ml (1 pt) with water

salt and plenty of black pepper
2 bay leaves (optional)

Dry-fry the mince, a little at a time and drain it. Transfer it to a large saucepan (or slow-cooker). Using the fat from the meat, or a little added oil, fry the onions until they are translucent, drain them and add them to the mince. Discard the remaining fat/oil. Make up the stock cubes with the water, add this to the mince, season and stir well. Put the pan on the stove and bring the mixture to the boil, stirring occasionally to ensure it doesn't stick, then either turn the heat down to very low and cover the pan, or transfer the contents to a slow cooker. Let it cook for 2 - 3 hours, checking occasionally that it isn't sticking.

To convert this basic savoury mince for other dishes:
- for Bolognese sauce – to beef mince, add 2 cloves of garlic, chopped and lightly fried, 3 - 4 tablespoons tomato paste and 1 teaspoon each of dried thyme and oregano, plus 1 tablespoon coarsely chopped fresh basil. (This sauce can also be used in lasagne.)
- for Chilli Con Carne – to beef mince, add 3 - 4 tablespoons tomato paste, 1 - 2 tins of red kidney beans and 1 - 2 teaspoons chilli powder.
- for Shepherds (lamb) or Cottage (beef) Pie, add 2 large carrots, cooked and roughly chopped.
- for Moussaka - to lamb or beef mince, add 2 cloves of garlic, chopped and lightly fried, 2 tablespoons tomato paste and 3 - 4 medium aubergines, cut into thick rounds and lightly fried and drained.

BURGERS

You can make burgers with any sort of minced meat, adding appropriate herbs and spices if you wish. For economy, substitute breadcrumbs for up to a quarter of the suggested meat content. This recipe will make 6 burgers.

250 g (8 oz) lean minced meat   salt and pepper
50 g (2 oz) onion, finely chopped   vegetable oil for cooking
2 tablespoons natural yoghurt

Mix the meat, onion, yoghurt and seasonings thoroughly, then divide the mixture into six equal parts. Form each into a ball, then lay it on a flat surface and press it into a flat round. To grill, brush the top of each burger with oil, invert it onto the grill pan and brush the top surface with more oil before grilling for 5 - 6 minutes each side. To fry, heat a shallow layer of oil in a frying pan and fry the burgers for 5 - 6 minutes each side. Serve in a bun, or on a plate with salad or chips.

MUSHROOMS

TO BUY

The choice of fresh mushrooms used to be whether to buy them as tightly closed 'buttons', larger 'closed cups' or big open 'flat' mature mushrooms. All of these are still available, in white or chestnut (thought by many people to have a better flavour), but now you can get more exotic cultivated mushrooms, and in some better supermarkets, wild mushrooms. The exotic cultivated mushrooms and wild mushrooms are considerably more expensive than the ordinary version, and which you choose will be dictated by your own taste or the recipe you are following. Both of the latter are also available in dried form.

As far as ordinary mushooms are concerned, the flavour develops as the mushroom matures. Buttons are attractive to look at but have little flavour, closed cups are still attractive with more flavour, open flats are full of flavour, but since the gills tend to be black, will colour the dish. They are normally used to stuff or fry on their own.

TO STORE

Fresh mushrooms should be used within 24 hours of purchase. If they are packed in plastic, remove this as soon as you get home. Store them in a paper bag in a cool place, but not a fridge, which will make them sweat. Mushrooms do not freeze well raw but can be frozen if lightly fried in butter, for up to 2 months.

Dried mushrooms should be stored in an airtight jar, and can be kept for many months.

TO PREPARE

Fresh cultivated or wild mushrooms should not be immersed in water as this makes them soggy and flavourless. Instead, wipe each one over with a piece of kitchen paper or a damp cloth to remove any soil. Trim off the ends of the stalks and slice or cut into quarters. Large open mushrooms for frying should have the stalk cut off near the head so they will lay flat in the pan.

Dried mushrooms – put them into a bowl and pour boiling water over them. Leave them to soak for 30 minutes, then lift the mushrooms out of the water, checking that no soil or other debris is clinging to them. Gently pour the soaking liquid through a sieve into another bowl, watching out for grit in the bottom of the bowl. This soaking liquid can be used as stock.

TO COOK

Although fresh mushrooms can be added to stews and cassseroles, it is best to fry them lightly first. They can also be roasted or grilled, in which case they need to be drizzled with a little oil to prevent them drying out. Otherwise, they can be fried and served on their own or with other fried food. Button mushrooms or small specimens are easiest to handle in the pan if they are sliced or quartered.

Use olive or another vegetable oil, or butter, duck fat, bacon fat or beef dripping, heating the fat before adding the mushrooms and tossing them quickly to seal them before turning the heat down. Fresh mushrooms can absorb a great deal of fat if you let them, so start with a little fat and keep them moving in the pan rather than add more fat. Drain them well before serving.

Dried mushrooms are best added to stews or casseroles, as they remain tough when fried.

MUSSELS

TO BUY

Mussels should be bought live from a reputable fishmonger, on the day when you intend to cook them. You will need about 2 kg (4 lbs) of mussels for 4 people.

TO CLEAN AND PREPARE

With a nail-brush, scrub each mussel under cold running water, and use a knife to help you pull off the stringy 'beard' and scrape off any barnacles. Throw away any mussels which are not firmly closed during this process as they are dead and thus could be dangerous to eat.

TO COOK

Mussels can be steamed or boiled in plain water, but the commonest way of cooking them is as follows. However you cook them, any which do not open during cooking should be thrown away as they could be dangerous to eat.

MOULES MARINIERE

2 kg (4 lbs) live mussels
2 tablespoons olive oil
2 cloves garlic, crushed
300 ml (10 fl oz) white wine
1 bouquet garni
salt and black pepper

300 ml (10 fl oz) water
  or fish stock
25 g (1 oz) butter
1 tablespoon finely
  chopped parsley

Prepare the mussels as above. In a very large saucepan, heat the oil and fry the garlic for 2 minutes over medium heat. Add the wine, bouquet garni, seasoning and mussels. Bring to the boil, cover the pan, and simmer for 5 minutes, shaking the saucepan at intervals. Using a slotted spoon, lift out the mussels and divide them between 4 deep soup plates. Add the water and butter to the pan, bring back to the boil and boil for 3 - 4 minutes until the liquid has reduced. Check the seasoning, pour the liquid over the mussels and sprinkle with parsley before serving.

NOODLES

TO BUY

Dried Chinese egg noodles are a yellowy colour, Cellophane noodles (also known as bean noodles) are translucent and off-white, while rice noodles are opaque and white. Most come in 225 g (8 oz) packets, which is enough to feed four people.

TO STORE

Store, in the packet, in a dry cupboard. Once the packet is open, place the unused noodles in a plastic bag or sealable box or jar. Leftover cooked noodles can be kept in the fridge in a plastic bag or sealed dish for 24 hours.

TO COOK

Bring plenty of water to boil in a large saucepan. Put in the sheets of noodles and stir until they have separated. Take the pan off the heat, cover it and let it stand for 5-6 minutes before draining the noodles in a colander. Very fine cellophane noodles need no more than soaking in boiling water for about 5 minutes.

Fine thread or rice noodles can be fried. Put the whole sheet of noodles into hot oil, wait for it to puff up and take it from the oil and drain it on kitchen paper. Sprinkle some salt on it before serving.

SINGAPORE NOODLES

100 g (4 oz) fine cellophane noodles

100 g (4 oz) coconut cream, broken into small pieces

120 ml (4 fl oz) hot chicken stock

1 tablespoon mild curry powder

1 tablespoon peanut or sesame seed oil

50 g (2 oz) button mushrooms, finely sliced

2 spring onions, finely sliced

50 g (2 oz) cooked chicken or ham, shredded

50 g (2 oz) small prawns

2 oz cooked peas

2 fresh green chilli peppers, finely sliced

2 eggs, beaten with 1 teaspoon sesame seed oil

Put the noodles in a large bowl and cover them with boiling water, then leave them to soak for 20 minutes. In a small bowl, dissolve the coconut cream in a few spoonfuls of the hot stock, then stir in the curry powder before adding the rest of the stock. In a wok or very large frying pan, heat the oil and lightly fry the mushrooms and spring onions. Add the chicken, prawns, peas and chillies and stir-fry for 2 - 3 minutes. Drain the noodles well and add them to the wok, stirring to mix them in before adding the curry sauce. Continue to stir-fry until most of the liquid has gone, then add the egg mixture, stirring constantly until the egg is cooked before serving.

NUTS

NOTE: Some people have an extreme allergic reaction to nuts (especially peanuts) in any form, which can cause them to go into a toxic shock attack which may kill them. For this reason, you should always ask whether diners are able to eat nuts before using them in recipes.

TO BUY

Nuts can be bought still in their shells, shelled and untreated, and roasted (with or without added salt). As cracking the shells is time-consuming, if you want nuts to cook with, it is best to buy them shelled, although they cost more. The most popular nuts for cooking are almonds, hazelnuts and walnuts, all of which are available in various forms. Almonds come whole with or without their skins, in halves, 'nibs' (small chunks), flaked (thin slices) or ground. Hazelnuts come whole, as halves or as smaller pieces, in either case raw or roast. Walnuts come whole, in halves, or smaller pieces, with the whole nuts the more expensive. You can also buy pecan nuts (like a small walnut), cashew nuts (delicious but very expensive) and pistachio nuts.

Buy nuts in small quantities, as they lose their flavour quickly and become rancid. Unshelled nuts will last longer than shelled nuts.

TO STORE

Unopened packets of nuts may be kept in a cool dry cupboard. Once opened, they should be used quickly, but can be kept in an air-tight box or jar for up to 2 weeks. Roast and/or salted nuts can be kept for 4 - 6 weeks.

Nuts in their shells will keep for up to 4 months.

See also separate entries for chestnuts, coconut and peanuts.

WALNUT SAUCE FOR PASTA

1 clove garlic
100 g (4 oz) shelled walnuts
2 tablespoons fresh white
   breadcrumbs
2 tablespoons milk

3 tablespoons oil (olive will do,
   but walnut is better)
4 tablespoons ricotta cheese
salt and pepper
grated Parmesan cheese for serving

This sauce is enough for 450 g (1 lb) pasta. Put everything except the seasoning and Parmesan in the processor and whizz it until it is smooth. If you do not have a food processor, use a pestle and mortar to crush the garlic and nuts before mixing in the rest of the ingredients thoroughly with a fork. Taste and season, then put it in a serving bowl for diners to add to their pasta. Hand the Parmesan separately for them to sprinkle on top.

OFFAL

TO BUY

Offal is a general term used for various internal organs – liver, kidneys, sweetbreads, tripe, brains, hearts. All offal should be moist and shiny - and fresh (should be eaten within 2 or 3 days of slaughter). Reject any which looks greenish, shiny, or smells unpleasantly strong.

TO STORE

You can freeze offal if it is absolutely fresh, but otherwise you should cook it on the day you buy it.

TO PREPARE AND COOK

To give a better texture, brains, sweetbreads and tripe should be soaked in cold water for 1-2 hours, then put in a saucepan of fresh cold water and brought to the boil, then simmered for a few minutes. Drain and rinse well before completing cooking. Brains can then be poached in a well-flavoured stock. Hearts and lambs' tongues are best when braised. Kidneys should be skinned, then cut in half to remove the gristly core. This is most easily done with scissors. They can be grilled, or can be sliced and fried in butter, as can sweetbreads.

SHERRIED KIDNEYS

25 g (1 oz) butter
1 clove garlic, crushed
1 small onion, chopped
4 lambs kidneys, skinned,
   halved and cored

1 tablespoon plain flour
1 teaspoon Worcestershire sauce
300 ml (10 fl oz) stock
2 tablespoons sherry
1 tablespoon chopped parsley

In a large saucepan, melt the butter and fry the garlic and onion for 4 - 5 minutes. Add the kidneys and fry them for 2 minutes, then stir in the flour. Add the Worcestershire sauce, the sherry and the stock gradually, stirring to prevent lumps. Bring the liquid to the boil then turn down the heat and cover the pan to simmer for 15 minutes, then for a further 10 minutes without the lid.

OILS

TO BUY

Buy oils in small quantities, as they lose their flavour quickly and become rancid. Olive oil is classified by its acidity level. First cold pressing (also called 'extra virgin') is the best, next is virgin, and finally 'pure' (which is a mixture of refined olive oil and some extra virgin oil). For cooking, pure or virgin oil is perfectly adequate. Extra virgin should be kept for salad dressings. You can also get Estate Bottled oils, which tend to be expensive, but each has its own individual flavour.

Walnut or hazelnut oils are expensive but have a wonderful flavour. Keep these strictly for salads.

Sesame seed oil can be used for salad dressing or cooking. It will tolerate very high cooking temperatures, as will peanut (sometimes called groundnut) oil.

Sunflower, safflower, corn (maize), grapeseed, soya or rape seed oils are all adequate for frying. Some people also find them adequate for salad dressings or making mayonnaise.

TO STORE

Oil should be kept in a cool dark dry cupboard, to prevent it going rancid. Don't keep it in the fridge as this will make it go cloudy.

ONIONS

TO BUY

For salads choose red onions or long thin spring onions. For cooking choose either big mild Spanish onions, or the medium sized yellow onions, which have a stronger flavour. Small silverskin onions can be used for pickling or cooking whole in casseroles. Shallots are small and intensely flavoured. Cooking onions should feel firm – reject any which feel soft.

TO STORE

Spring onions can be kept in the fridge for 3 - 4 days. Other onions and shallots will keep for several months if you buy them in autumn and keep them in a cool dry airy place, such as hanging in a net in a shed. Sliced or chopped onion can be frozen for up to 6 months.

TO PREPARE

Onions make you cry because their fumes irritate your eyes. The trick is to peel and cut them in front of you instead of immediately under your face, and to peel the whole batch before you cut the tops and root ends off them, thus delaying the point at which you release the fumes. Small onions can be difficult to peel unless you immerse them briefly in boiling water.

To slice an onion, leave the root end on after peeling, then cut the onion in half from top to bottom, lay the flat surface down on the chopping board and start slicing at the top end, working your way down to the roots, which you then throw away.

To chop an onion, start as above, but before slicing, first make a series of cuts parallel to the one that cut the onion in half, lay it down, then slice through it from top to roots several times. Slice as before, and it will fall into small cubes as you cut.

TO COOK

Onions can be roasted, baked, stewed or fried, or added to any savoury dish. When frying onions, do so gently, as they burn easily and then taste bitter. If the recipe tells you to fry them without browning, add salt at the beginning of cooking time.

FRENCH ONION SOUP

75 g (3 oz) good beef dripping
  or olive oil
½ teaspoon sugar
1 kg (2 lbs) onions,
  halved and sliced
2 cloves garlic, crushed

1 litre (2 pts) beef stock
salt and lots of black pepper
4 thick slices of French bread, toasted
100 g (4 oz) Gruyère cheese, grated

In a large saucepan, melt the dripping, add the sugar, onions and garlic and fry them until they are starting to brown. Don't worry if the sugar starts to stick to the bottom of the pan – this is normal. Add the stock gradually, stirring well to loosen the sugar, then add salt to your taste and generous amounts of freshly ground black pepper. Bring to the boil, then turn down to simmer for about 1 hour. Sprinkle the cheese over the toast and put it under the grill to melt and crisp while you pour the soup into four bowls. Float one piece of cheesy toast in each bowl before serving.

ORANGES

(MANDARINES, CLEMENTINES, SATSUMAS, TANGERINES, ETC)

TO BUY

Sweet oranges come in many varieties and many pricing methods. The larger fruits, such as navels (which means that the orange has a navel-like end opposite the stem, and no pips) tend to be priced individually, and medium-sized fruits can either be sold by weight or in net bags. Large fruits often have very thick skin, so what seems like a bargain may be less so when you remove the peel. Smaller orange-relations, such as tangerines or satsumas, appear in the shops in late autumn. They have loose segments, and thus are only suitable for eating in the hand. There are also various orange/tangarine crosses, with the physical attributes of the large oranges but the additional sweetness of the tangarine. One of the best of these is the Ortanique.

Whichever type is involved, the fruits should be unblemished and the skins should appear full and have a shiny surface. Slight blemishes and skin which is beginning to wrinkle is acceptable in oranges for juicing, provided the price has been adjusted downwards.

Seville oranges are available in late January, and are only suitable for making marmalade, as they are quite bitter.

TO STORE

Oranges will keep for many weeks at room temperature, and can also be frozen, either whole or as slices or juice.

TO PREPARE

The outer layer of orange peel (the thin orange coloured layer) can be used in many ways, so it is worth removing it before you peel the orange. First scrub the orange to remove any wax or ink, dry it with a soft cloth, then use a vegetable peeler or zester to take off strips of peel. These can be used straightaway, dried in a very slow oven, or stored in a jar of sweetened alcohol, until you need some to add to a stew or a bouquet garni.

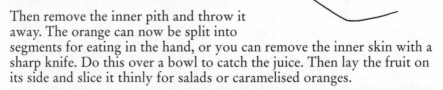

Then remove the inner pith and throw it away. The orange can now be split into segments for eating in the hand, or you can remove the inner skin with a sharp knife. Do this over a bowl to catch the juice. Then lay the fruit on its side and slice it thinly for salads or caramelised oranges.

TO COOK

The most common way of using oranges in cooking is to use the juice for sauces, but this is a classic Italian dessert.

CARAMELISED ORANGES (for 4 people)

4 large navel oranges	300 ml (10 fl oz) water
1 stick of cinnamon	350 g (12 oz) granulated sugar

Remove the zest from two of the oranges with a zester and set it aside. Peel all the oranges and slice them thinly as above. Put them and any juice into a serving bowl with the cinnamon stick. Put half of the water and all the sugar into a saucepan and bring it to the boil, stirring constantly with a wooden spoon, then turn down the heat and let it reduce to a golden-brown. Boil the rest of the water, **then cover both hands well as the next stage will spit**, and slowly pour the boiling water into the caramel, stirring until the mixture has softened. Pour about three-quarters of this over the sliced oranges, and leave it to cool before putting the dish in the fridge to chill. Meanwhile, return the rest of the syrup to the heat and put in the orange zest. Stir them in and leave them to cook and the liquid to reduce again. When the zests are candied, and the liquid is all gone, remove the pan from the heat and leave to cool. Arrange the candied zests over the oranges just before serving.

PANCAKES

See Batter (page 34) for basic batter recipe.

TO COOK
Use a 16 cm (7") or 23 cm (9") frying pan, ideally nonstick. Heat it on medium heat for a minute, then put in a little butter, lard, or sunflower oil, swirling the pan to distribute the fat evenly. Ladle or pour enough batter into the pan to cover the base, tilting the pan to spread the batter evenly. Cook over medium heat for about 1 minute, until the underside is golden-brown. Using a spatula, turn the pancake and cook the other side for about 30 seconds before turning out.

These pancakes can be used for sweet or savoury dishes.

TIP: Start by making fairly thick pancakes – thin ones require a little practice.

TO STORE
Pancakes can be stored, layered between sheets of greaseproof paper and sealed into a plastic bag, in the fridge for up to 48 hours, or in the freezer for up to 6 months.

TO SERVE
Pancakes can be flat with lemon juice and sugar, jam, maple syrup, apple purée or other sweet flavourings handed separately for diners to add themselves, or with these flavourings spread on each pancake which is then rolled before serving. You can serve them with ice cream or whipped cream.   Alternatively, you can fill them with a savoury filling such as chicken or prawns, pour a white sauce over the top, then brown them under the grill for 5 minutes.

PARSNIPS

TO BUY

If possible, choose small parsnips rather than enormous ones, as these latter will have tough cores. They should feel firm and heavy for their size, and the skin should not be wrinkled or bruised. The top should be intact, and the bottom should taper away to a thin root. Where the top and bottom have been trimmed excessively, I suspect this to be a way of tidying up tired specimens.

TO STORE

Parsnips can be stored for several days indoors, but after that they tend to dry out and wrinkle. If you have somewhere dry outside where you can store them, they will keep for 4 - 6 weeks.

TO PREPARE

Cut off the tip and stem end of each root, then peel them. Cut them in half lengthways, then into quarters. Long parsnips can be cut once more to make shorter pieces. Big or old parsnips should have the tough core cut out.

TO COOK

Tender young parsnips can be steamed for 8 - 10 minutes and served with a white sauce or mashed. Older parsnips can be boiled before mashing on their own or with potato. To roast parsnips when cooking a joint, first blanch them in boiling water for 5 minutes, then drain them and place them round the joint, basting them with fat. They will need to roast for 30 - 40 minutes.

PASTA

TO BUY

You need approximately 100 g (4 oz) pasta per person. Choose the shape of pasta for the type of sauce you will be serving with it – runny sauces are best with shapes such as shells or penne, which will retain more sauce.

TO STORE

Store, in the packet, in a dry cupboard. Once the packet is open, keep the unused pasta in a plastic bag or sealed box or jar. Leftover cooked pasta can be kept in the fridge in a plastic bag or sealed dish for 24 hours.

TO COOK

Bring plenty of water to boil in a large saucepan, and keep it at a fast boil during the cooking process. Add salt to your taste, then add the pasta a little at a time, to prevent it sticking. With long spaghetti, lower it slowly into the water, coiling it round the pan as it softens.   Dried pasta takes

10 - 15 minutes to cook, fresh pasta takes 2 - 3 minutes to cook. Pastas made with egg, including filled pastas such as ravioli, take a little longer than other types, and should be stirred gently until the water returns to the boil. Check the time recommended on the packet and test a little piece towards the end of the cooking time. Whether fresh or dried, pasta should be served 'al dente', which means 'resistent to the teeth'. As soon as it is ready, drain it immediately, as leaving it to stand in hot water continues the cooking process and it will go soggy.

Retain some of the cooking liquid, as you may want to dilute the sauce before serving.

PASTRY

There are five types of pastry, each suitable for different purposes. Short crust pastry is for tarts, pies or quiches, puff (or flakey) pastry is for vol au vents or pie tops and some sweet pastries, suet pastry is used for steamed puddings, filo (or phyllo) pastry is a very thin pastry used for wrapping savoury or sweet food, and choux pastry is used to make sweet items such as eclairs or profiteroles.

TO BUY
All except choux pastry can be bought ready made and chilled or frozen. Frozen pastry, especially pre-rolled sheets of short-crust pastry, is very convenient and easy to use.

TO STORE
Home-made pastry can be stored in the refrigerator, wrapped in clingfilm or a plastic bag, for 2 - 3 days. Pastry, either in blocks or pre-shaped tart or quiche bases, can be frozen for up to 6 months.

TO MAKE AND COOK PASTRY

SHORT-CRUST PASTRY

100 g (4 oz) plain flour   cold water
pinch salt
50 g (2 oz) fat –
   butter, lard, block (not soft)
   margarine, or a mixture

This recipe will make enough pastry to line a standard 23 cm (9") pie dish. If you want to cover the pie as well, use 150 g (6 oz) flour and 75 g (3 oz) fat. Sift the flour and salt into a mixing bowl. Cut the fat into small cubes and rub it in with your fingers, lifting the mixture as you rub, to incorporate air and make the pastry lighter. Continue until all the fat has been rubbed in and the mixture has the texture of fine breadcrumbs.

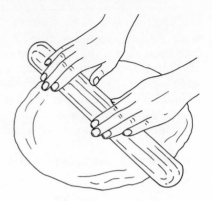

(At this stage, if you add as much soft brown sugar as there is fat, you have crumble topping, which can be spread over fruit to make a fruit crumble.) Sprinkle 2 or 3 tablespoons water over the mixture and use a knife to mix it, adding more water and finally using your hands to mix it to a smooth ball of dough. At this stage it helps to give the pastry a rest, so wrap it in clingfilm and put it in the fridge for 20 minutes.

Sprinkle a little flour on your rolling surface and gently roll out the pastry to the desired shape, turning it through 90 degrees after every couple of passes with the rolling pin. Always roll away from you, and roll out your shape a little bit larger than the tin it will bake in.

Cooking times will vary according to the recipe, but in general pies with pastry on top and on the bottom (called double crust) will need about 30 minutes in an oven heated to 200°C/400°F/ Gas Mark 6. It is important that double crust pies go into a pre-heated oven, as otherwise the bottom will not cook properly.

ROUGH PUFF PASTRY

450 g (1 lb) plain flour
pinch salt
450 g (1 lb) fat –
    half lard, half block (not soft)

margarine, straight from
the fridge
300 ml (10 fl oz) very cold water

Sift the flour and salt into a mixing bowl, then grate the fat into it, stopping every so often to mix it in using a knife. Then pour in the water and continue to mix with the knife until you have a rough lump of dough. Sprinkle a little flour on your rolling surface and turn the dough out onto it. Use your hands to form the dough into a flat-topped rectangle, then gently roll it out to an oblong about 30 cm (12") long and 20 cm (8") wide. (Ideally you should hold the rolling pin at the extreme ends, so your hands are not directly over the pastry.) Now roughly mark the oblong into three equal sections, then fold one over the middle and the other over the first. Press the edges together with the rolling pin to trap the air inside. Roll it back to the oblong shape and repeat the folding twice more. Then give the pastry a long rest in the fridge before rolling it out to use it.

Puff pastry needs a hotter oven than shortcrust pastry, 230°C/450°F/ Gas Mark 8.

CHOUX PASTRY

75 g (3 oz) plain flour
pinch salt
150 ml (5 fl oz) water

50 g (2 oz) butter, in small cubes
2 eggs, size 3, beaten

Preheat the oven to 220°C/425°F/ Gas Mark 7 and line 2 baking sheets with greaseproof paper. Sift the flour and salt into a bowl.

Put the water and butter into a saucepan and bring it to the boil. Take the pan off the heat and tip in the flour, then beat the mixture with a wooden spoon until it has thickened enough to come away from the sides of the pan.

Put the pan back on the heat and cook it, stirring, for 2 - 3 minutes. Turn off the heat and let the mixture cool for 10 minutes before beating in the egg, a little at a time. The mixture should end up at a dropping consistency and glossy.

For buns or profiteroles, use a tablespoon to drop dollops of the mixture onto the baking sheet, leaving sufficient room for expansion between them. For eclairs, transfer the mixture to a piping bag and pipe lengths of mixture onto the baking sheets. This amount of pastry should make 32 profiteroles or 16 eclairs. Bake for 20 - 25 minutes, until the buns are well risen and golden brown. Take them out of the oven, make a small slit in each for the steam to escape and return them to the oven for 2 - 3 minutes to dry out the insides. Spread them out on a wire rack to cool completely before filling. (For eclairs or profiteroles use real custard or whipped cream as a filling, for savoury fillings use chopped chicken or prawns in a white sauce, or a mixture of cream cheese and herbs.)

PÂTÉ

TO BUY

Pâté is made from chopped meat or fish, and comes in three 'grades' – coarse (sometimes called terrine) where you can see big lumps of meat, ordinary which is fairly smooth, and very fine (sometimes called mousse). Meat or poultry pâtés normally incorporate liver, but fish pâtés do not. Which type you buy is a matter of taste, but in general you should only buy pâté in small quantities as it soon goes off.

TO STORE

Bought pâtés should always be kept in the fridge, for 2 - 3 days unopened, no more than 2 days once opened. Home-made pâtés can be kept in the fridge for up to a week before they are started, provided that you have 'sealed' them with a layer of melted butter.

TO SERVE

Terrines can be served by the slice, on a plate with a garnish of salad. Pâté can be served by passing the dish for diners to help themselves, and is usually served with hot toast.

SIMPLE CHICKEN LIVER PÂTÉ

250 g (8 oz) chicken livers
250 g (8 oz) unsalted butter
1 shallot, very finely chopped

2 tablespoons brandy
salt and black pepper

Cut the chicken livers into quarters and fry them in half of the butter for 5 minutes, turning them to make sure they are well cooked. Drain them and place them in a liquidizer or food processor. Briefly fry the shallot, then add the brandy to the pan and stir well, scraping the pan to get all the bits of liver off. Add this mixture to the processor and whizz until it is smooth, then transfer it to a deep dish, making sure that there are no air-holes underneath. In a clean pan, melt the rest of the butter and pour it over the top of the pâté. Leave it to cool, then put it in the fridge to chill before serving.

PEACHES AND NECTARINES

TO BUY

The best time to buy fresh peaches and nectarines is in summer, when they are harvested in France, Italy and Spain. Although peaches may be available at Christmas, they tend to be mealy. White-fleshed peaches are expensive but have the best flavour. The main difference between peaches and nectarines is that a peach has a furry skin while a nectarine has a smooth skin. Nectarines are rarely mealy, whereas peaches which have been picked too soon are often mealy. Whichever you buy, they should be firm but not hard, and should not have any soft patches or bruises. They can be used interchangeably in recipes.

TO STORE

Peaches can be kept at room temperature for several days, but should be handled gently as they easily bruise.

TO PREPARE

Due to the possibility of pesticide residues, peaches should be rinsed under a cold tap, and ideally peeled before eating. When they are really ripe, the skin will come off easily with the assistance of a sharp knife. Otherwise you may need to immerse them briefly in boiling water before peeling. To remove the stone, cut the fruit all round its circumference, then twist the two halves in opposite directions. One half will come away from the stone easily, but you may need to wiggle the stone a little before it parts from the other half. If necessary, the halves can then be sliced.

TO COOK

Peaches are usually poached. Halve them, place them in a saucepan with just enough water to cover them, add 1 tablespoon sugar, bring the water to the boil then turn it down to simmer, covered, for 10 minutes. Remove the skins after they have cooled.

Peaches can also be baked. Halve or slice them, then put them in a baking dish and bake at 190°C/375°F/ Gas Mark 5 for 20 - 30 minutes. For each 450 g (1 lb) peaches, you will need approximately 150 g (6 oz) sugar.

After cooking, peaches can be served either hot or cold, with some ice-cream or Greek yoghurt.

PEANUTS

NOTE : Some people have an extreme allergic reaction to peanuts in any form, which can cause them to go into a toxic shock attack which can kill them very quickly. For this reason, you should always ask whether diners are able to eat peanuts before using them in recipes.

TO BUY

Peanuts come either in their shells (which should not rattle when shaken), or loose. Loose peanuts are usually roasted and may still be in their red skins, or skinless and salted. For cooking, buy them without salt. They also come as prepared snacks, coated and fried.

Peanut butter is available in smooth or chunky form, with or without added salt. For many cooking purposes, it can be substituted for whole peanuts, and because it keeps longer may be a better buy.

TO STORE

Peanuts in their shells can be kept for 4 - 6 weeks in a cool place. Unsalted nuts can be kept in an airtight jar for 3 - 4 weeks, salted nuts for 2 - 3 weeks. Peanut butter should be stored in the fridge once opened, but will keep for many months.

TO PREPARE

Peanuts are easily removed from their brown shells. Just crush the shells between your fingers and thumb. The red inner skin should then be removed, and the easiest way to do this is to roast the nuts for about 10 minutes in a dry roasting pan in a medium oven, then tip them out onto a clean tea-towel and rub them with a corner of the towel to remove the skins.

Where the recipe calls for the nuts to be crushed, place them in a plastic bag and crush them with a rolling pin. They can also be broken up or even puréed in a food processor, but you may need to add some liquid.

TO COOK

Peanuts can be used in many dishes, including curries, stir-fries, and as a meat substitute in recipes such as meat loaf. They are also used to make a sauce for satays (skewers of chicken or pork).

PEANUT SAUCE FOR SATAYS

6 tablespoons crunchy
  peanut butter
3 tablespoons olive oil
2 tablespoons dark soy sauce

juice of 1 lime or lemon
½ teaspoon chilli powder
25 g (1 oz) coconut cream
water

Put all the ingredients except the water in a saucepan and heat gently, stirring well. Add water gradually until you have a thick sauce, turn down the heat and simmer for 10 minutes before serving hot or cold with satays.

PEARS

TO BUY

To cook, you need a hard pear, but for eating raw, it is best to buy underripe pears and let them ripen at home. The change from perfectly ripe to overripe and mealy is so quick that what seems like a good pear when you buy it in the morning can be horrid by the same evening. Williams' or Comice are dependably good varieties for cooking or dessert eating, but the elongated Conference is also good and less likely to turn mealy. Buy them when they are still hard and green and check them every day until they are turning greenish gold and feeling a little softer.

TO STORE

Pears should be kept at room temperature.

TO PREPARE

All pears should be cored and peeled before eating. If preparing them for cooking, you need to slide each piece into acidulated water to prevent it going brown.

TO COOK

Pears should be gently simmered in a large saucepan, in either sugared water or sweetened red wine. In either case, use 120 ml (4 fl oz) liquid and 25 g (1 oz) sugar, plus a half cinnamon stick for each pear. For quartered pears, simmer for 15 - 20 minutes, for whole pears simmer for 25 - 30 minutes.

PEAS

TO BUY

Fresh green peas – the pods should be bright green, and should pop open easily when pressed. They should squeak when pressed against each other, and should feel full. Silver 'netting' on the outside of the pod is an indication of maggots inside.

Mange-tout or sugar peas – as above, but the pods should not be full or they will be tough.

Dried peas – for soups, choose green peas or yellow split peas. For 'mushy' peas, you can buy packets of peas which include soaking tablets which speed up the cooking process.

Tinned peas – the choice is 'garden' peas, either full size or petit pois, neither of which are as good as the frozen versions; marrowfat, which may be mashed and called 'mushy'; and pease pudding. Both marrowfat peas and pease pudding are quite good from tins.

Frozen peas – quality varies from brand to brand, but in general frozen peas are better than tinned or elderly fresh peas.

TO CLEAN

You should not need to clean dried peas, but it is wise to check that packets do not include small stones. Fresh green peas only need to be rinsed before cooking.

TO STORE

Fresh peas should be used soon after buying. Keep them in a cool place, but not a fridge which will make them flabby and difficult to shell. There is little point in freezing fresh peas, as the results will never be as good as commercially frozen peas, which are podded and frozen in the field (in mobile processers) usually within an hour of picking. Bought frozen peas can be kept in the freezer for up to 12 months.

Store dried peas in the packet, in a dry cupboard. Once the packet is open, keep the unused peas in a sealed box or jar. Dried peas keep a long time but deteriorate after 6 months.

TO PREPARE

Fresh green peas – holding the pod over a large bowl or colander, press the seams until the pod pops open, then run your thumb along the peas to push them out of the pod. Discard the pods.

Mange-tout or sugar peas – break off the stalk and pull it down one side to remove the string. Do the same with the tip. Leave the pods whole, or cut them diagonally before cooking.

TO COOK

Fresh green peas – drop the peas into boiling salted water and cook for 5 - 10 minutes, depending on the size of the peas. Some people like to add a spoonful of sugar and/or some mint leaves.

Mange-tout peas – boil the whole pods, as above, or steam them for the same time. They can also be stir-fried, or eaten raw.

Dried peas should be soaked overnight, then boiled in fresh water. Peas are cooked when they are tender right through, and they should then be drained, unless you are making 'mushy' peas, in which case they should be cooked until they turn to mush.

PEAS IN THE FRENCH STYLE

900 g (2 lbs) peas in their pods
50 g (2 oz) butter
3 - 4 spring onions, roughly chopped
1 medium carrot, peeled and finely chopped

2 small lettuces, shredded
150 ml (5 fl oz) chicken or vegetable stock
salt and pepper
1 teaspoon sugar (optional)

Shell the peas. Put them with the butter, spring onions, carrot, lettuce and about half of the stock in a saucepan. Bring the stock to the boil, then turn down and simmer for 5 minutes. Taste and season, add more stock if necessary, cover the pan and simmer for a further 10 minutes. Check that the peas are cooked, simmering for a further few minutes if necessary, before serving.

PEPPERS (Capsicums)

See Spices for white and black pepper

TO BUY

Green peppers are red peppers which haven't yet matured to the stage where they colour up. They are not as sweet as red peppers. Red, yellow, orange (and even dark purple) peppers all taste the same, so you only need buy a selection of colours for their beauty.

TO STORE

Peppers can be kept in the fridge for 4 - 5 days, but will become flabby after that. Ideally you should use them on the day you buy them, while they are at their best.

TO PREPARE

Sweet peppers – to core a sweet pepper, hold it in one hand and cut deeply round the stalk with a paring knife. Pull the core out by the stalk. This should bring most of the seeds with it, but any loose seeds can be shaken or rinsed out.

To peel peppers, roast them in the oven at 230°C/450°F/ Gas Mark 8 or under the grill until the skin blackens, then place them in a sealed paper bag for 15-20 minutes. This steams them and loosens the skin so that you can scrape it off with a knife.

For stuffing, choose peppers that are all the same size and shape. If you can get them with flat bases, leave the stem in place and cut the tops off about 1 cm (½") down. This gives you a 'lid'. Otherwise, cut them in half lengthways, including the stem. Remove the seeds but leave the stems in place. Lay the halves flat for stuffing.

Chilli peppers – ideally you should prepare chilli peppers wearing rubber gloves. Be careful not to touch your face or eyes until you have washed your hands, as well as the knife and cutting board. Cut off the stem end before slicing the chilli into rings or strips. The seeds are also very hot, and you may prefer to remove them.

TO COOK

Sweet peppers can be fried, roasted, grilled or barbecued as well as being served in salads. Chilli peppers are usually added to savoury dishes.

STUFFED PEPPERS (for 4)

4 red or green peppers
  (or 2 of each)
1 medium tomato, peeled,
  deseeded and chopped
1 small onion, peeled and
  finely chopped
1 - 2 tablespoons olive oil

100 g (4 oz) long grain rice, precooked
25 g (1 oz) raisins, plumped
  in hot water
25 g (1 oz) pine nuts (optional)
½ teaspoon dried oregano or thyme
salt and black pepper
boiling water

Preheat the oven to 180°C/350°F/ Gas Mark 4. Prepare the peppers by slicing them in half lengthways (then you can give each diner one red half and one green half), removing the seeds and laying them in a large baking dish. In a frying pan, lightly fry the tomato and onion in the oil. Take the pan off the heat and add the rice, raisins, pine nuts, oregano and seasoning. Mix well and divide the filling between the pepper halves. Pour about 2 cm (1") boiling water into the dish, put it into the oven and bake for 45 - 50 minutes. Keep an eye on the peppers, and if the filling seems to be drying out, cover the dish with a layer of foil.

PICKLES AND CHUTNEYS

TO BUY

There are so many types of pickle or chutney available that it is very much a case of 'buy what you like'. However, it is worth studying the list of ingredients to check the type of vinegar which has been used. You may find that those which say 'pickling condiment' or 'acetic acid' rather than 'vinegar' will have an unpleasantly acidy 'bite'.

TO STORE

Once opened, purchased or home-made pickles and chutney should be kept in the fridge and consumed within 3 - 4 weeks.

TO PREPARE

To make simple pickles, all you need is some vinegar, some spices, and the vegetables, so you can make your own pickles without filling the house with the smell of boiling vinegar. Making chutney involves the same process as making jam, where you stir while the mixture cooks, so you should not embark on chutney making unless you are prepared for the time and the smell.

The rule with pickle is that the smaller the pieces of vegetable, the sooner the pickles will be ready to eat. If you want spices, you can either buy a ready-prepared mixture called 'pickling spice', or mix your own. The basic mix includes black and white peppercorns, mustard seeds, cloves, and mace, but you can add chilli peppers, dill seed, or whatever the recipe calls for. In general the spices need to be boiled in the vinegar, but you can also buy ready-spiced pickling vinegar, which avoids this (rather smelly) process.

You can use either malt or wine vinegar, but it is best to avoid the rather harsh 'pickling condiment'. Malt vinegar is usually brown, but it is also available in a clear distilled form. Many recipes suggest that the vinegar should be boiling when it is poured over the vegetables, but this tends to make them go soft quickly, so it is better to use cold vinegar.

To make simple chutneys, you need some onion, some vinegar and some spices and some fruit such as apple or vegetable such as tomato or pumpkin. Most people make chutneys in the summer when fruit or vegetables are cheap, or when they have a glut in the garden.

Whether making pickles or chutney, the jars should be sterilised as for jam (see page 11), and they should ideally be proper preserving jars, as the vinegar can react badly with metal lids and make them rust quickly.

QUICK PICKLED ONIONS

sufficient preserving jars to
  hold 4 litres (8 pts) pickle
2 kg (4 lbs) small pickling
  onions or shallots

2 litres (4 pts) malt vinegar
25 g (1 oz) pickling spice
  (optional)

Sterilise the jars, apportion the spices between the jars, and pour enough vinegar into them to one-third fill them. Peel the onions, dropping each one straight into the jars as it is done. As each jar fills with onions, top up the vinegar. You should end up with 1 cm (½") vinegar covering the onions. Close and seal each jar. Each day for 2 weeks, invert the jars to spread the spices, then put them away in a dark cupboard for 6 - 8 weeks before using them.

TOMATO CHUTNEY

1½ kg (3 lbs) tomatoes
  (ripe or green) roughly chopped
2 onions, finely chopped
100 g (4 oz) sultanas
100 g (4 oz) dark brown sugar
  (demerara)

1 teaspoon allspice
1 teaspoon powdered ginger
1 teaspoon mixed spice
1 teaspoon salt
black pepper
150 ml (5 fl oz) malt vinegar

You will need 4 - 6 jam-jars for this chutney. Mix all the ingredients in a large saucepan or preserving pan, bring it to the boil then turn it down to a fast simmer, stirring regularly, until it thickens. (About 1 hour). Take it off the heat and let it cool slightly before bottling. Let the jars cool completely before putting on the lids, then put the chutney away to mature for 3 - 4 weeks before using.

PIES

Pies, whether sweet or savoury, and whether or not they have a pastry base, always have a top which can be pastry, scone dough, or mashed potato. If it has a pastry base but no top, it is a tart - but just to confuse everyone, some tarts are called pies in America, so the classic American Pumpkin Pie is what we would call a tart.

TO BUY

You can buy both sweet and savoury pies fresh or frozen, cooked or uncooked, so here it is a case of buying what you like and following the instructions on the box.

TO STORE

Home-made pies with pastry cases, once cooked, should be kept in the fridge and eaten within 24 hours. You can freeze cooked or uncooked pies, in both cases, well wrapped in foil. If cooked, put them in the freezer as soon as they have cooled down. Meat pies can be kept frozen for 3 - 4 months (chicken for only 1 month), fruit pies up to 6 months. Savoury pies with mashed potato topping are best frozen without the topping.

TO PREPARE AND COOK

'Pie' can be used to describe so many things that the best advice I can give is to refer to the relevant sections here (e.g. Pastry, Apple, etc) and make a few general comments:

* when making savoury pies with a mashed potato topping, always cook and mash the potato after preparing the filling. Cold mashed potato is very difficult to handle.
* rough the top of mashed potato toppings with a fork before putting the pie into the oven, to give an attractively browned topping.
* fruit pies usually have a base as well as a top of pastry. They can be made with raw or cooked fruit, but they cook more quickly with hot cooked fruit, which reduces the risk of the top burning.
* the same applies to vegetable pies.
* if the pastry on your pies seems to be in danger of burning before the filling is cooked, place a piece of foil over them to complete the cooking time.
* meat pies should always be made with pre-cooked meat, to ensure that the meat cooks thoroughly.
* double-crust pies (those with pastry underneath as well as on top) should always have the filling put into them very hot, and go into a very hot oven at the start of cooking.
* painting the bottom crust with egg-white prevents it getting soggy from damp fillings.
* keep a stock of frozen ready-rolled pastry sheets and tinned fruit pie fillings for quick and easy desserts.

PINEAPPLE

TO BUY

Ripe pineapples should smell sweet and fruity. Gently tweak one of the inner leaves of the plume, which should come away easily when the fruit is ready. Reject pineapples which feel soft or have brown patches.

TO STORE

Unripe pineapples will ripen at home at room temperature. Ripe pineapples can be kept for 2 - 3 days, also at room temperature. Once cut, pieces of pineapple should be kept in a lidded bowl in the fridge. You can sprinkle them with sugar if you wish.

TO PREPARE

The easiest way to prepare a pineapple is first to cut off both ends, then cut downwards to remove the peel. Slice into rounds.

Don't be tempted to add add fresh pineapple to jellies or mousses. They contain an enzyme which acts against the gelatine and prevents setting.

TO SERVE

Pineapple slices can be served cold with cream or ice-cream, or can be grilled or roasted to serve with gammon steaks, or as a hot pudding.

PIZZA

TO BUY

Pizzas are available in both frozen or fresh form, both ready to cook. You can also buy pizza bases and add your own toppings. Often the least expensive and easiest way to have a really tasty pizza is to buy a simple ready-to-cook pizza with no more than tomato sauce and cheese on it, then add more toppings.

TO STORE

Follow the storage instructions on the packet with ready-to-cook pizzas. Once cooked, pizza leftovers should be kept in the fridge for 24 hours. There is little point in precooking pizzas to eat later unless for a picnic.

TO COOK

True pizza bases are made of a bread-like dough, which is shaped and topped before baking. However, you can also make a good imitation 'pizza' using slices of bread, scone dough, or puff pastry. If you do not want to make the dough from scratch, buy ready made and rolled pizza bases.

PIZZA DOUGH (enough for 1 large pizza)

120 ml (4 fl oz) lukewarm water	plus a little more for kneading
½ teaspoon granulated sugar	pinch salt
1½ teaspoons dried yeast	1 teaspoon olive oil
225 g (8 oz) strong white flour,	1 egg, beaten

Put about half of the water into a small bowl and stir in the sugar and yeast. Set aside to froth up for 10 minutes. Add the salt to the flour and stir it in, then make a well in the centre and pour in the frothed yeast, the egg and the rest of the water. Using your hands, mix everything together in the bowl, working it until it forms a ball of dough. Turn this out onto a lightly floured surface and knead it for 10 minutes. When ready it should feel springy and elastic.

Now put the dough into an oiled plastic bag and leave it to stand in a warm place for about an hour, or until it has doubled in size. Turn it out onto the floured surface again and knead it for 5 minutes before shaping it to fit your baking tin and adding the toppings.

Preheat the oven to 220°C/425°F Gas Mark 7. Bake the pizza for 15 - 20 minutes. It is best to place the pizza directly onto the oven shelf or invert a baking tray in the oven, preheat it, then slide the pizza onto the hot tray. Check that the base is cooked right through by lifting it with a spatula and looking underneath.

PIZZA TOPPINGS
Pizza toppings usually start with a layer of tomato sauce. If you want to make your own, use the recipe on page 139, halve the quantities given and cook the sauce until it is thick. Spread this over the pizza base before adding your other favourite toppings. These could include grated or thinly sliced cheese (Mozarella and Parmesan are traditional), sliced and pre-fried onions, sliced green and red peppers, olives, mushrooms, bacon or ham, and slices of salami or pepperoni sausages.

PLUMS AND PRUNES

TO BUY
There are many varieties of plums available at various times during the year. As well as the red or purple plums, there are greengages which come in early summer, and tiny dark purple damsons which come in early autumn. Most plums and greengages can be eaten raw, but damsons are very tart and are only used for jam or pies.

Plums should have a dusty-looking bloom on their skins, to show that they haven't been handled too much, but many imported plums have been washed and the bloom has gone. It is best to buy unripe plums and let them ripen at home, as they bruise easily once ripe and soon go off. Prunes are dried plums. They are almost black in colour, and have an intense flavour. You can buy them tinned, in syrup, or dried, either to soak yourself or pre-soaked and ready to eat. These latter are the best sort if you want them to stuff pork. Dried prunes have usually been de-stoned.

TO STORE
Plums should be kept at room temperature. They should keep for up to a week, but it is wise to check them every day. They can also be frozen –

halve them and remove the stones, then 'open' freeze them on a tray, transferring them to a bag or box once they are solid. They can be kept in the freezer for up to 6 months.

TO PREPARE

To eat raw, plums only need washing. For cooking, they should be halved and stoned. Some varieties come away from the stone easily, others have to be cut away. Cut one plum all the way round its circumference, deep enough to feel the stone, then twist the two halves in opposite directions. If one half comes off easily, you will see whether you have a loose stone, in which case cut all the others the same way. If not, cut them all round from top to bottom, starting at the natural seam, then slip the knife round the stone to remove it. Some plums may have a blemished area at the bottom of the stone. This can be cut away and the rest of the plum used. Prunes need to be soaked for 2 - 3 hours, either in plain boiling water, or in weak China tea.

TO COOK

Stew plums with sugar in a lidded saucepan, adding 2 - 3 tablespoons of water at the beginning to prevent sticking. You will need 100 - 150 g (4 - 6 oz) sugar to 450 g (1 lb) of plums, depending on their tartness and your own taste. Damsons may need even more sugar.

PORK

TO BUY

To roast, choose leg or shoulder. To grill or fry, choose chops, cutlets, or fillet (also known as tenderloin). For stews and casseroles, choose belly or spare rib chops.

TO STORE

All raw meat should be wrapped and stored in a refrigerator, for up to 72 hours. Pork can be frozen for up to 9 months, except belly which should only be frozen for 6 months and mince which should only be frozen for 3 months.

TO PREPARE

Roasting joints and gammon steaks may need a little trimming to remove excess fat. Snipping through the edging fat on steaks with kitchen scissors at 2 cm (1") intervals will prevent them curling up during cooking. Otherwise, just rinse the meat under cold water and dry with kitchen paper before cooking.

TO COOK

Pork can be casseroled, grilled, fried, or roasted. For casseroles, it is advisable to remove as much as possible of the fat before cooking, and sometimes you will also need to remove liquid fat which has risen to the surface during cooking.

Fillet or tenderloin are the most expensive of pork cuts, but the tenderest. They can be roasted (with stuffing if desired) or sliced thinly and pan-fried. Leg, loin or hand of pork are good roasting joints with plenty of skin for crackling. Roast pork at 180°C/350°F Gas Mark 4 for 45 minutes per ½ kilo (1 lb).

For good crunchy crackling, the skin must be dry and well-scored. Get the butcher to do this for you, or do it yourself with a very sharp knife (a hobby knife is perfect). Just before cooking, sprinkle salt over the skin and rub it in. Cook for the first 20 minutes at 230°C/450°F Gas Mark 8, then reduce the heat as above.

POTATOES

TO BUY

Buy the right sort of potato for the way you intend to cook them – different varieties have different cooking properties, and if you try to boil a floury baking potato you'll end up with soup, just as trying to bake a salad potato will give you a hard soapy result.

For mashing, choose Cara, Golden Wonder, King Edward or Wilja; for salad, choose Charlotte, Jersey Royal, Pink Fir Apple or Ratte; for chips, choose Arran Comet, Desiree, Maris Piper, Pentland Dell or Wilja; for baking, choose Cara, Wilja, Desiree or King Edward.

TO CLEAN

Wash potatoes just before cooking them, using a soft scrubbing brush to remove stubborn dirt.

TO STORE

Potatoes must be stored in the dark, or they will develop green patches which can be poisonous.

TO PREPARE

For mashing or roasting, peel potatoes as thinly as possible (much of the goodness is just under the skin), and remove any blemishes or 'eyes' (the indentations which shoots grow from) before cooking. For baking, just scrub the skin and prick it with a fork to prevent it bursting. New potatoes can be scraped to remove the skin, but this is not essential.

TO COOK

To boil potatoes, they should be cut into even sized pieces, then put into a saucepan with enough cold salted water to cover them, brought to the boil and turned down to simmer for 15 - 20 minutes. Test them with a sharp knife to check that they are done right through, then drain them straight away. (Do not automatically throw the cooking water away - it makes a good base for stock or soups.)

If the potatoes are to be mashed, return them to the cooking pan after draining, add a few knobs of butter or some warm milk, and mash them with a large fork or a potato masher. Some people add white pepper. Stop mashing while the potato is still fluffy – over-mashing leads to a gluey mess (as does using a food processor).

To roast potatoes, proceed as for boiling, but drain the potatoes as soon as the water has boiled. Lay them in a roasting pan (round the meat if you are cooking a joint) and baste them with fat – either the fat from the joint, or your preferred vegetable oil. Put the tin back in the oven for 45 minutes before lifting the potatoes out with a perforated spoon.

To bake potatoes, clean them, prick them with a fork, then lay them on the middle shelf of a hot oven. Bake for 1 - 1 ½ hours, until they are soft right through. You can speed up the cooking time by pushing a long metal skewer through the middle of each potato. If you have a gas stove, you can buy a special clay pot (from kitchen shops) which allows you to 'bake' potatoes on top of the stove.

PRAWNS

TO BUY
Raw prawns are grey, cooked prawns are pink. Normally, only tiger prawns are sold raw. When bought fresh, both will still have their shells on.   Frozen prawns should be thawed at room temperature. In emergencies, they can be thawed quickly by immersing them in hot water, but this may result in a loss of flavour.

TO CLEAN
Rinse the prawns under cold water and remove the shells, starting with the head. With raw prawns, you may have to peel the sections of shell off the body one at a time, with cooked prawns the shells come off more easily. There may be a dark vein running along the middle of the back, if so make a small cut with a sharp knife and pull this vein out, starting from the head end.

TO STORE
Fresh prawns should not be stored for more than 24 hours. Frozen prawns may be kept for up to 1 month.

TO COOK

Prawns can be stewed, grilled or barbecued, fried or stir-fried. They take only minutes to cook, and should not cook for too long as this makes them tough and dry.

PRAWN COCKTAIL (serves 4)

4 tablespoons mayonnaise
(page 95)
2 tablespoons tomato ketchup
2 teaspoons lemon juice
225 g (8 oz) cooked and
peeled prawns
salt

8 lettuce leaves, shredded
paprika
1 lemon, cut into 8 wedges
lengthways
8 slices brown bread and butter,
crusts trimmed off and cut
diagonally into quarters

Mix the mayonnaise, tomato ketchup, and lemon juice together well, then fold in the prawns. Add salt to taste. Arrange the shredded lettuce in 4 serving bowls and divide the prawn mixture between them. Sprinkle a little paprika on top, add 2 wedges of lemon to each serving, and serve with the bread and butter on a side plate.

PUMPKINS AND SQUASHES

TO BUY

Although you can use the flesh from the inside of a Hallowe'en lantern pumpkin, pumpkins tend to have rather watery flesh and very little flavour, so for most purposes it is better to buy squash, which has a denser, nutty tasting flesh. Acorn or Rolet squash are quite small and mild flavoured, Butternut or Kabocha are larger and have a distinct chestnut flavour. 'Vegetable spaghetti' is a type of squash which looks like a long pale melon, and which has stranded flesh which looks like spaghetti. There are many other varieties, but these are the ones you are most likely to find in supermarkets. On street markets you can sometimes buy slices of larger types. All should be firm and feel heavy, without serious blemishes on the skin (although some scabbing is natural in some varieties).

TO STORE

All pumpkins and squashes will keep for several months until they are cut open. After cutting, wrap them in clingfilm and keep them in the fridge for 3 - 4 days. Puréed pumpkin or squash can be frozen for up to 12 months.

TO PREPARE

For stuffing or baking as a half, you only need to remove the seeds and the strings which they nest in. For other purposes you should also remove the skin. In this case, it is easiest to cut the squash into small pieces first, then cut the skin from each piece. Some of the larger varieties have very tough skin – to get into them, put the whole thing inside a plastic bag and drop it onto the floor so that it breaks open. Vegetable spaghetti should not be peeled before cooking.

TO COOK

Never boil pumpkin or squash, unless you are making soup. The flesh will waterlog, and you can't drain it adequately. It is better to steam pieces, or to wrap halves in foil and bake them at 180°C/350°F/ Gas Mark 4 for 30 - 40 minutes before scraping out the flesh. It can be served mashed on its own or with potato (or potato and apple), or roast like potatoes round a joint of meat. For stuffing, you can either wrap the squash in foil and roast it before stuffing it, or stuff it and bake it in a tin with 5 cm (2") water in the tin.

Vegetable spaghetti – prick the skin a few times with a skewer, then immerse the whole thing in boiling water and boil for 20 - 30 minutes. Drain, let it cool, then cut it open, remove the seeds, and use a fork to tease the strands loose. Serve these with a pasta sauce, or a vinaigrette dressing.

QUICHES AND FLANS

Quiches are open-topped savoury tarts, made with a pastry base and a filling based on eggs and cream. Flans are always sweet and can be made with a base of short crust pastry, special flan pastry called pâté sucré (which is difficult to handle and not recommended for new cooks) or sponge.

TO BUY

You can buy both sweet flans and savoury quiches fresh or frozen, cooked or uncooked, so here it is a case of buying what you like and following the instructions on the box. You can also buy ready-made sponge bases for sweet flans.

TO STORE

Home-made flans and quiches, once cooked, should be kept in the fridge and eaten within 24 hours. Both are better frozen cooked than uncooked; in both cases open frozen as soon as they have cooled down, then well wrapped in foil. Quiches can be kept frozen for 3 - 4 months, flans (pastry or sponge based) 1 - 2 months depending on the filling. However, in general it is better to freeze the bases (baked blind if pastry) and fill them when needed.

TO PREPARE

Simple sponge-based fruit flans are quick and easy to prepare. You need a sponge base, which can either be bought or made like one half of a Victoria sponge (see page 48) with a layer of the centre removed. Then you need some fruit, which can either be raw (strawberries, raspberries, peaches) or lightly poached (peaches, pears) or tinned. Poached and tinned fruit should be well drained. Arrange the fruit in an attractive pattern straight onto the sponge base, then mix a little boiling water with some strawberry or apricot jam and use this as a glaze to cover the fruit and hold it in place. You can also put a layer of sweet custard on the base before arranging the fruit.

Pastry-based flans or tarts come in two types – those which are made in the same way as sponge flans, and those which are made with a filling which includes eggs and cream, and baked after filling. The latter can be made with a ready-baked base, but this is not necessary. (This also applies to quiches.)

BASIC QUICHE

1 recipe short crust pastry
  (see page 111)
4 eggs, beaten
300 ml (10 fl oz) double cream
50 g (2 oz) grated cheese
  (Cheddar or Gruyère)
salt and pepper

225 g (8 oz) other filling
  (lightly fried onion, steamed
  asparagus or broccoli,
  strips of ham, spinach,
  mushrooms, courgette, etc.)
a little milk for the pastry edges

Preheat the oven to 180°C/350°F/ Gas Mark 4. Roll out the pastry and use it to line a 20 cm (8") flan dish. Mix the eggs, cream, cheese and seasoning together. Spread the other filling round the base of the pastry and pour in the egg mixture. Paint the exposed edges of the pastry with a little milk, then bake for 30 - 40 minutes, until a skewer inserted in the middle comes out clean.

BASIC SWEET EGG-MIX FLAN

1 recipe short crust pastry
(see page 111)
  4 eggs, beaten
300 ml (10 fl oz) double cream
75 g (3 oz) caster sugar
up to 225 g (8 oz) other filling
  (chopped fresh fruit such

as strawberries, peaches or figs,
or dried fruit such as prunes
or apricots, ground almonds,
pine nuts etc.)
a little milk for the pastry edges
a little icing sugar

Preheat the oven to 180°C/350°F/ Gas Mark 4. Roll out the pastry and use it to line a 20 cm (8") flan dish. Mix the eggs, cream, and sugar together. Spread the other filling round the base of the pastry and pour in the egg mixture. Paint the exposed edges of the pastry with a little milk, then bake for 30 - 40 minutes, until a skewer inserted in the middle comes out clean. Let the flan cool then sift some icing sugar over the top.

RABBIT

TO BUY

Many people are put off by the strong flavour of wild rabbit. Farmed rabbit does not have this strong flavour, and tastes much like chicken. A medium sized rabbit about 1 kg (2 lbs) will be sufficient for two people.

Rabbit can be bought in ready-to-cook portions from supermarkets or butchers, or as whole animals from specialist butchers. Wild rabbits are a grey-brown colour, farmed rabbits are usually white, but may be black. Ask the butcher to skin it for you (it will already have been 'paunched' (gutted) and unless you want the head, tell him to remove it, as a skinned head can be rather off-putting.

TO CLEAN

Wash the meat well, ensuring that there is no fur sticking to it.

TO STORE

Raw rabbit should be kept in the fridge for no more than 48 hours before cooking. It can be frozen for up to 6 months.

TO COOK

Rabbit meat tends to be dry, and so is usually casseroled or stewed. When used to make a pie, stew the rabbit first and remove the bones, and include some streaky bacon or belly pork, in the proportion 4 parts of rabbit to one of bacon.

RADISHES

TO BUY

Salad radishes are small, usually red or red-and-white, and sold in bunches. Daikon (or Mooli) radishes are much larger and always white. All should feel firm and have a shiny skin.

TO STORE

Radishes should be kept in the fridge for 1 or 2 days, but no longer, as they will become flabby.

TO PREPARE

Radishes which have become slightly flabby can be refreshed by soaking them in iced water for an hour. If they are really flabby and looking wrinkled, throw them away. Otherwise, wash them gently in cold water, and top and tail them. When they are to be eaten with the fingers, you can leave some of the stem on to form a useful handle, and serve them with a bowl of sea salt for diners to dip them into.

RASPBERRIES

TO BUY
Fresh raspberries should feel firm when gently touched, and there should be very little, if any, juice in the bottom of the punnet.

TO CLEAN
Raspberries should be rinsed just before use. If there are holes in the bottom of the punnet, rinse the whole punnet under a gently running cold tap, shake off the worst of the water and tip the berries onto double thickness kitchen paper. Check that there are no bits of leaf or other small items sticking to the berries before transferring them to a saucepan to cook. If you intend to use the berries raw, pick out the best specimens and roll them on the paper to dry them off.

TO STORE
Fresh raspberries should not be stored for more than 24 hours, as they start to deteriorate as soon as they are picked. Raspberries are best used raw, but they can be frozen for up to 12 months, either individually or in boxes. However, they can only be used for cooking or puréeing with cream after defrosting, as freezing makes the tissues collapse.

TO COOK
Raspberries are mostly liquid, and need hardly any water when cooking. Put 1 - 2 tablespoons of water in the bottom of the pan, add the berries and sugar and set the pan over medium heat. Cover the pan, but check it every couple of minutes to make sure there is sufficient liquid, adding water by the tablespoonful if the pan is dry. You will need about half the weight of sugar to berries, but start with half that amount, as the sweetness of the berries themselves can vary.

RHUBARB

TO BUY
Tender pink stems of early rhubarb have been forced by growing in the dark. Later in the season the stems will be thicker and darker. Reject any which are floppy, split or bruised.

TO STORE

Fresh rhubarb can be stored in a cool place for several days. If possible, stand the stems, root end down, in cold water, as this will help keep it fresh. Once prepared, it can be kept in the freezer, either cooked or chopped and packed loose in bags, for up to 12 months.

TO PREPARE

Forced rhubarb does not need peeling, merely wiping with a damp cloth. Later in the season, tough skin may need to be peeled. In either case, cut off the root and leaf ends before cutting the rest of the stem into sections. **Note that rhubarb leaves are poisonous and should never be eaten.**

TO COOK

Stew rhubarb with sugar in a lidded saucepan, adding 2 - 3 tablespoons of water at the beginning to prevent sticking. You will need 100 - 150 g (4 - 6 oz) sugar to 450 g (1 lb) of rhubarb, depending on its tartness and your own taste. Some people like to add some orange juice to reduce the acidity which clings to your teeth after eating rhubarb.

RICE

TO BUY

For most savoury dishes, choose long-grain rice, such as basmati. For risotto, choose a rice such as arborio which is labelled as being suitable for risotto. Cook 50 g (2 oz) raw rice per person. For sweet rice puddings, buy short-grained 'pudding' rice. 2 tablespoons of raw rice will make enough pudding for 4 people.

TO CLEAN

You should not need to clean rice, but if you buy it in bulk without a reliable label, it is wise to check that it has no small stones with it. However, some people believe you should rinse and soak Basmati rice, for about 15 - 30 minutes, before cooking to remove the excess starch which can make it sticky.

TO STORE

Store, in its packet, or in a sealed box or jar, in a dry cupboard. Leftover cooked rice can be kept in the fridge in a plastic bag or sealed dish for 24 hours.

TO COOK

There are many ways to cook rice for savoury dishes, but this is the simplest and most reliable. Use a liquid measuring jug to measure the rice, then add two times as much cold water as rice. For two people, you will need 1 teacupful of uncooked rice, and 2 teacupsful of water. Put rice and water into a saucepan and stir it to separate the grains. Add 1 teaspoon of salt, and bring the water to the boil, then turn the heat right down and cover the pan. Cook for about 20 minutes, then check that all the water has been absorbed, cooking for a further couple of minutes if it has not. Take the pan from the heat and let it stand for 5 minutes, then fluff up the rice with a fork before serving.

RICE PUDDING

25 g (1 oz) butter
2 tablespoons pudding rice
600 ml (1 pint) milk

2 - 3 tablespoons sugar
3 - 4 drops vanilla essence
(optional)

Preheat the oven to 160°C/325°F/Gas Mark 3. Butter an ovenproof dish. Rinse the rice and put it in the dish with the sugar, milk and vanilla essence. Stir gently. Dot the rest of the butter on top. Put in the middle of the oven and cook for 2 ½ hours. Some people like to stir the skin into the pudding at intervals while it cooks.

BAKED RICE PILAU

This is an adaptation of a classic Persian dish, where the most honoured guest is served the crispy bits from the bottom of the dish.

(125g) 5 oz raw long-grain rice
600 ml (1 pt) salted water
50 g (2 oz) sultanas

250 g (8 oz) butter
1 medium onion, thinly sliced
25 g (1 oz) flaked almonds

Cook the rice in the salted water in the usual way. (You can also use left-over rice for this recipe.) Preheat the oven to 180°C/375°F/ Gas Mark 4. Stir the sultanas into the rice and transfer it to a deep, lidded, oven-proof dish. In a frying pan, melt the butter and fry the onions until they are golden brown, then drain them and pour all the butter over the rice. Stir it in, level the top and spread the fried onions over it. Put the lid on and bake the rice for 30 minutes, then take off the lid, sprinkle the almonds over the top and bake without the lid for a further 5 - 10 minutes for the almonds to toast (keep an eye on them in case they start to burn). Serve on its own or with a meat dish, making sure that every diner gets some of the onions and the almonds.

SALADS

TO BUY

You can buy many different made-up salads from delicatessen counters in supermarkets, but none of them are as good as the ones you make at home. The trick with salads is to choose ingredients which have contrasting textures and flavours, and also a pleasing set of colours. It's very much a matter of experimentation and deciding what you like, but some suggestions and tips follow.

TO STORE
Some salads, such as potato salad, will keep for 2 - 3 days, others should be eaten on the day they are prepared. In general it is the salads which contain mayonnaise which can be kept longer. All should be covered with clingfilm and kept in the fridge.

TO PREPARE
Each ingredient suggests by its shape and form how it should best be cut – for instance while you can cut potato into cubes, apples look best in slices with their skin on, oranges look best cut in round slices across the segments, and ordinary onions are best sliced thinly and separated into rings, while spring onions can be sliced straight or diagonally.

Ingredients which discolour when cut, such as apples, should be cut and added at the last moment, having been dipped into lemon juice. Leftover rice and pasta can be used in salads, but should be consumed within 24 hours of cooking, as should chicken.

POTATO SALAD
Use new potatoes or a variety with waxy flesh, such as Jersey Royal or Ratte. They accept the dressing best when they are hot, so cut them up before cooking them, drain them, and mix the dressing in straight away. The dressing can be mayonnaise or a simple vinaigrette. Some finely chopped spring onions, chives, and chopped parsley or mint make a good addition or garnish.

WALDORF SALAD
Bite-sized pieces of apple, celery and walnuts (some people use peanuts) in a mayonnaise dressing.

ORANGE AND ONION SALAD
Use medium sized oranges, peel them and cut off all the pith and the outer skin of the segments, then slice them thinly into rounds, saving any juice. Choose an onion about the same size as the oranges, peel it and slice it thinly, then separate the rings and sprinkle them on top of the orange. Pour the juice on top. Alternatively, substitute thinly sliced green peppers for the onion.

COLESLAW
Use half of a small white cabbage, 1 - 2 carrots, and some mayonnaise. Shred the cabbage finely, peel the carrots and cut them into batons, and mix with some mayonnaise and, if you like it, a little wine vinegar. You can add a crisp apple, some celery cut very thin, or anything else crunchy.

Some other possibilities to start you thinking:
Fennel, with orange and watercress (no dressing), or with Mozarella cheese and celery and a dressing of lemon juice and olive oil.

Green Peppers stuffed with cream cheese and chives, or sliced with thin slices of raw button mushrooms and a simple vinaigrette dressing. Haricot or butter beans with fresh green beans and red kidney beans or chick peas and a simple vinaigrette dressing, or broad beans with black olives and chopped basil. Beefsteak tomatoes, thickly sliced, then layered with slices of Mozarella cheese and sprinkled with fresh basil leaves.

SALMON

TO BUY

Now that salmon is farmed, fresh salmon is no longer the expensive luxury it used to be. It is easy to cook, and normally acceptable even to people who dislike fish. For parties, buy a whole salmon. Otherwise, buy salmon 'steaks' or fillets. For dishes which involve breaking up the flesh, such as pies or fish-cakes, buy tail portions which are cheaper.

Smoked salmon can be bought as whole sides which you will have to slice yourself, or ready sliced in small quantities. Reject slices which look dry at the edges.

TO CLEAN

Fresh whole salmon should have been cleaned (and gutted) by the fish-monger. All you have to do, as with portions, is to rinse the fish under a cold tap and remove any small bones before cooking.

TO STORE

Fresh salmon should be kept in the fridge for no more than 48 hours before cooking. Smoked salmon slices can be stored in the fridge for up to 72 hours. Vacuum-packed smoked salmon can be kept for several weeks as long as the seal is intact. Fresh salmon can be frozen for up to 2 months.

TO COOK

Salmon steaks or fillets can be grilled, baked or poached. Whole fish can be poached, if you have a large enough fish kettle, (some cookshops or branches of supermarkets such as Asda keep fish kettles to lend to customers) or baked, wrapped in buttered foil. One way round the problem of not having a big enough dish for the whole fish is to cut the fish in half across its 'waist', cook the two halves separately, skin them and reassemble the fish on a serving dish, then use very thin slices of cucumber, arranged like fish scales, to cover the whole fish and disguise the join.

To poach a whole salmon, measure the thickness of the fish (side to side) then place it on its side in a fish kettle or deep baking tin and cover it with boiling water or a mixture of one part white wine to three parts water. Cover the kettle/dish and cook on a medium hot burner for 10 minutes for each 2 ½ cm (1") of its thickness. (Start timing when the liquid boils.) Test for doneness by inserting a knife into the fish just behind its head and lifting a little flesh to see if it is cooked right through. Lift the fish out of the kettle and leave to drain before serving.

Tip: If you do not have a fish kettle with a special device for lifting the fish, fold some foil to four thicknesses and place this under the fish, leaving enough hanging over the sides to lift it out when it is cooked.

SANDWICHES

TO STORE

Once made, sandwiches should be kept airtight, or the bread will harden and start to curl. Plastic bags, clingfilm or foil are all suitable wrappers, either for individual sandwiches or platefuls. Once made, store sandwiches in a cool place, or the fridge. Provided that the fillings do not contain egg, mayonnaise or salad, you can make sandwiches in batches, then wrap them individually and freeze them for up to 2 months. This is a good way of using up bread and other ingredients as well as speeding up the daily task of packing lunch boxes for school or office.

TO PREPARE

If using butter, soften it before spreading, or the bread will tear. The fresher the bread, the softer the butter should be. When making large quantities of sandwiches, it is worth softening the butter until it is quite sloppy, and using a pastry brush to spread it.

Cut the bread into slices, or use a ready cut loaf, and lay the slices out in pairs, so they will fit back together as they come off the loaf. Spread the butter or margarine, starting with the slice furthest away from your spreading hand, so you do not trail your hand over the slices that have been spread. Then spread any other soft fillings (such as pickle) on alternate slices, add harder fillings (such as slices of cheese) on top, and cover with the other slice. If you want crustless sandwiches, remove the crusts after putting the sandwich together.

FILLING SUGGESTIONS

- Cheese and pickle (buy 'sandwich' pickles, which have smaller pieces and spread more easily).
- Cream cheese, with chopped nuts, dates, sultanas, chopped spring onions, well-drained pineapple, banana and honey, watercress, mustard and cress, or other salad leaves.
- Hard-boiled egg with mayonnaise, mustard and cress.
- Salad, prawn, and prawn cocktail sauce.
- Salmon, smoked mackerel, or smoked trout, all flaked and mixed with cream cheese or a little horseradish.

- Slices of cold meat – beef with horseradish or mustard, ham with mustard, chicken with curry mayonnaise, corned beef with pickle, salami, pâté, etc.
- Bacon, lettuce and tomato (known as 'BLT').
- Peeled and thinly sliced cucumber – traditionally on very thinly sliced brown bread.
- Tinned asparagus, well drained – traditionally on very thinly sliced brown bread, rolled round one piece of asparagus.

SAUCES

There are three simple sauces – white, brown, and tomato – and one slightly more difficult sauce – Hollandaise. All these recipes make 300 ml (10 fl oz) sauce, and all can be converted into other sauces with the addition of one or more ingredients.

TO PREPARE
WHITE SAUCE

15 g (½ oz) butter
15 g (½ oz) plain white flour
300 ml (10 fl oz) milk

salt and white pepper
nutmeg (optional)

In a saucepan over a gentle heat, melt the butter, stir in the flour, and cook for 1 minute, continuing to stir. Take off the heat and add the milk, a little at a time, stirring to prevent lumps forming. Season to your taste before returning to the heat. Bring to the boil, then simmer, stirring, for 2-3 minutes before transferring to a serving dish.

VARIATIONS ON WHITE SAUCE
For a classic béchamel sauce, start by putting the milk in a saucepan with 1 slice of onion, 1 bay leaf, 6 black peppercorns and a blade of mace. Bring it to boiling point, take it off the heat, cover it and leave it for 10 minutes to infuse. Strain the milk and continue as above. For a parsley sauce, stir in 2 tablespoons chopped parsley before serving. For a cheese sauce, stir in 50 g (2 oz) grated Cheddar cheese and a ½ teaspoon of mustard powder (optional) during the simmering process.
For an onion or mushroom sauce, gently fry 1 small chopped onion or 50 g/2 oz finely sliced mushrooms) in a little butter for 5-10 minutes and stir this into the sauce while it simmers.

BROWN SAUCE

50 g (2 oz) carrot, chopped
25 g (1 oz) onion, chopped
25 g (1 oz) celery, chopped
300 ml (10 fl oz) beef or veal stock
bouquet garni (a sprig of parsley,
    a bay leaf, 2-3 sprigs thyme)

25 g (1 oz) butter
50 g (2 oz) tablespoons plain flour
1 teaspoon double concentrated
    tomato purée (sometimes 'paste')
salt and pepper

Put the chopped vegetables into a saucepan with the stock and the bouquet garni. Bring this to the boil, cover the pan and simmer for 25-30 minutes. Strain and dispose of the solids. In a clean saucepan, melt the butter, stir in the flour, and cook for 1 minute, continuing to stir. Take off the heat and add the tomato purée and the stock, a little at a time, stirring to prevent lumps forming. Season to your taste before returning to the heat. Bring to the boil, then simmer, stirring, for 2-3 minutes before transferring to a serving dish.

VARIATIONS ON BROWN SAUCE
For a brown mushroom sauce, gently fry 50 g (2 oz) finely sliced mushrooms in a little butter for 5-10 minutes and stir this into the sauce at the simmering stage with 2 tablespoons medium sherry. For a Madeira sauce, gently fry 1 small onion, chopped, in a little butter for 5-10 minutes, and stir this into the sauce at the simmering stage with 3 tablespoons Madeira wine.

TOMATO SAUCE

4 tablespoons olive oil	salt and pepper
1 small onion, chopped	2 teaspoons fresh chopped,
2 cloves garlic, crushed	or 1 teaspoon dried, herbs –
2 kg (4 lbs) ripe tomatoes,	basil, oregano, thyme, or a mixture
peeled and roughly chopped,	1 teaspoon sugar (optional)
or the equivalent in tins	

In a medium saucepan, heat the oil and fry the onion for 6-7 minutes, then add the garlic and fry another 2-3 minutes. Add the tomatoes, bring to the boil, then simmer for 20 minutes. (If you want a smooth sauce, strain and return the liquid to the pan.) Add the herbs, salt and pepper to your taste, and simmer for a further 20-30 minutes until the sauce reaches your preferred thickness. Taste and adjust the seasoning, adding the sugar if necessary.

HOLLANDAISE SAUCE

Hollandaise is made from butter and cooked egg yolks, and it must be cooked very gently if it is not to turn into scrambled eggs.

2 egg yolks	75-100 g (3-4 oz) butter at
salt	room temperature
3 tablespoons white wine vinegar	white pepper

Heat a saucepan of water until it is barely simmering. Take a bowl which is big enough to sit on top of the saucepan without touching the water, and (before putting it on the saucepan) put into it the egg yolks and a pinch of salt, then whisk in the vinegar. Soften the butter to a creamy texture. Put the bowl over the simmering water and whisk the egg yolk mixture until it is thick and creamy – about 3 minutes. Gradually add three-quarters of the butter, whisking as you do so. Taste, adjust the seasoning, and if you think the sauce is too vinegary, gradually whisk in the rest of the butter. The finished sauce should be just thin enough to pour. If the sauce starts to curdle, take it off the heat, add an ice-cube and continue whisking until it becomes smooth again. Serve immediately, or remove the saucepan from the heat, cool the water by adding some cold until it is warm rather than hot, and replace the bowl over the warm water.

TO STORE SAUCES

Hollandaise sauce should not be stored. White, brown, or tomato sauces, or any of their variations – transfer to a dish and press a piece of greaseproof paper onto the surface to prevent a skin forming. You can keep them in a refrigerator for two days. Return to a saucepan and heat through gently, stirring to prevent lumps, before serving. Sauces containing milk should not be frozen as they will separate. Others can be frozen for up to 4 months.

SAUSAGES

TO BUY

The term 'sausages' can include salami and other types of sausage which can be eaten without cooking, but here we mean sausages which you buy raw and have to cook yourself. Even so, there is tremendous variety, ranging from the simple pork sausage to those containing beef, lamb, venison, or mixtures, plain, spicy, herbed, or almost any other combination.

There is also tremendous variation in the price you have to pay for sausages, but the general rule is that the more meat they contain, the more they will cost. Cheaper sausages are bulked out with rusk or breadcrumbs, and may be contained in artificial 'casings' rather than the natural casings made of intestines. They may also contain various additives and preservatives.

Some supermarket chains now sell a better type of sausage, and many towns have specialist sausage shops which only use fresh ingredients. These sausages are more costly, but well worth the extra.

TO STORE

Sausages should be kept in the fridge, and used within 48 hours of purchase. They can also be kept in a freezer for up to 2 months.

TO COOK

Sausages can be shallow fried over a medium heat, or roasted at 180°C/350°F/ Gas Mark 4. In either case, add sufficient fat or water to the pan to prevent them sticking, and turn them several times during cooking. Do not prick the skins – this was only necessary during war-time when poor quality casings were used and they otherwise exploded. Cooking time is largely a matter of taste, but sausages containing pork should always be well cooked (15 - 20 minutes for chipolatas, 25 - 30 minutes for full-sized sausages).

Sausages can also be grilled or barbecued, but it is difficult to cook them right through without burning the outside, unless you first simmer them for 5 minutes.

Once cooked, sausages can be added to stews or casseroles.

SAUSAGE ROLLS (makes 24)

½ recipe puff pastry (see page 112)
450 g (1 lb) chipolata sausages of
   your favourite type, half-cooked

1 small egg,
   beaten with 1 tablespoon milk

Preheat the oven to 220°C/425°F Gas Mark 7. Roll out the pastry thinly. Slit the sausage skins and remove the sausagemeat. Lay the skinned sausages out on the pastry, end to end, about 1 cm (½") from the edge of the pastry. Roll the pastry over the sausages and keep rolling until the pastry overlaps by 1 cm (½"). Mark this point with a knife and unroll the pastry a little. Cut the pastry at the point you've marked, paint some egg mix on the overlap with a pastry brush, then roll it up again and press the join firmly. Repeat as many times as needed to use up all the sausages and pastry. Cut the rolls into your preferred length, transfer them to a baking sheet and paint the tops with more egg mix before baking them for 20 - 25 minutes. Serve them straightaway, or let them cool and reheat them for serving later. See also Charcuterie and Cooked Meats.

SCONES

Simplest of all the baked goods for teas or snacks, scones are easily made. They can be plain or fancy, with currants or cheese added, or the dough can be used to top fruit instead of pastry (called a cobbler rather than a pie.) You can also buy them ready made.

TO COOK

225 g (8 oz) self-raising flour
pinch salt

50 g (2 oz) butter
or margarine milk to mix

Lightly dust 2 baking sheets with flour and preheat the oven to 200°C/425°F/ Gas Mark 7.

Sift the flour and salt into a mixing bowl and rub in the butter. Add enough milk to make a soft dough and turn this out onto a floured surface. Roll the dough out gently, or pat it into shape (it is important to handle scone dough lightly) until it is about 2 cm (1") thick. Cut rounds (with a pastry cutter or inverted glass) or squares and place them on the baking sheets. Bake for about 10 minutes on the top shelf of the oven. They are cooked if lightly pressing the sides with your fingers does not leave a mark. Put them on a wire rack to cool completely.

To make currant scones, add 50 g (2 oz) currants after rubbing in the fat. To make cheese scones, add 50 g (2 oz) grated cheese after rubbing in the fat.

SOUPS

TO STORE

Home-made soups can be stored, covered, in the fridge for up to 3 days, or frozen, for up to 3 months. To reheat soups, either pour them into a saucepan and cook over a medium heat, stirring until they are the required heat, or heat individual bowlsful in the microwave by cooking on HIGH for 2 - 2 ½ minutes.

Vegetarians can substitute vegetable stock for meat stocks.

When the recipe calls for the mixture to be liquidized, you can do this in a liquidiser or food processor, or by pressing it through a sieve with a wooden spoon.

LEEK AND POTATO SOUP

25 g (1 oz) butter
3 leeks, cleaned and roughly
 chopped, both white and
 green parts
3 large potatoes, peeled and
 roughly chopped
1 litre (2 pts) chicken
 or vegetable stock

salt and pepper
2 - 3 sprigs parsley, finely
 chopped for garnishing
4 tablespoons single cream or
 yoghurt, for garnishing

Melt the butter in a large saucepan, add the leek, put the lid on and cook for 8 - 10 minutes, stirring at intervals. Add the potato and stock and bring the mixture to the boil, turn down to simmer and taste before seasoning. Simmer 10 - 15 minutes or until the vegetables are soft right through. Take the pan from the heat and let the mixture cool for about 15 minutes before liquidising it until it is smooth. Return it to the saucepan, check the seasoning, and reheat before serving, garnished with cream and/or parsley.

TOMATO SOUP

1 kg (2 lbs) fresh tomatoes,
  or the equivalent in tins of
  Italian plum tomatoes
25 g (1 oz) butter
1 medium onion, peeled and
  finely chopped
1 clove garlic, crushed

1 tablespoon plain flour
2 tablespoons double
  concentrated tomato purée
  (sometimes labelled 'paste')
600 ml (1 pt) vegetable stock
salt and pepper
2 teaspoons caster sugar

Peel, skin and deseed the fresh tomatoes (see page 151), or sieve the
tinned tomatoes to get rid of the seeds. Melt the butter in a large saucepan
and gently fry the onion and garlic until they are translucent. Stir in the
flour, then the tomato purée, and add about half of the stock, a little at a
time, stirring to avoid lumps. Add the tomatoes and the rest of the stock,
season, and taste before adding sufficient sugar to take away any acidy
taste. Bring to the boil, then simmer for 8 - 10 minutes before serving.

MINESTRONE

Minestrone is an infinitely variable soup, which you can make with more
or less what you have available and want to use up. The meat content (if
desired) can be some chopped bacon, left-over mince or the remains of a
Bolognese sauce, and the vegetable content, while it needs a base of
onion, potato, and bean, can include almost any other vegetable. The
pasta content can be left-over cooked pasta, broken bits of pasta from the
bottom of the packet, or other shapes of your choice. Start by following
this recipe, then experiment to create your own version.

3 tablespoons olive oil
4 rashers streaky bacon,
  chopped
1 medium onion, peeled
  and chopped
2 cloves garlic, crushed
1 carrot, peeled and chopped
1 stick celery, chopped
1 medium potato, peeled
  and chopped
1 small green cabbage, shredded

50 g (2 oz) dried beans, soaked and
  pre-cooked
optional – other vegetables of your
  choice - tomatoes,
  peppers, leeks, green beans, etc
1½ litres (3 pints) stock
2 teaspoons dried herbs –
  thyme and/or oregano
salt and pepper
50 g (2 oz) dried pasta
grated Parmesan cheese to serve

In a large saucepan, heat the oil over medium heat, add the bacon, onion
and garlic and fry until the onion is translucent. Add the other vegetables,
the stock, and the herbs. Bring to the boil, then simmer until the
vegetables are almost cooked. Taste and season, bring back to the boil and
add the pasta, continuing to cook until the pasta is done. (To speed up the
process, you can cook the pasta separately and add it to the soup when
the vegetables are cooked.) Check and adjust the seasoning before serving
with Parmesan for diners to add themselves.

SPICES

TO BUY

Spices do not last indefinitely, so it is best to buy them loose in small quantities, ideally from a shop which has a regular turnover of stock, such as a Chinese or Indian grocer. Purists say you should buy them whole and grind them yourself, but this is not always practical, except for black pepper. If you do want to grind your own spices, toast them for 3 minutes in a heavy-based saucepan without fat or liquid before grinding.

You are most likely to need cloves, ground cinnamon and ground ginger, as well as white and black pepper and nutmeg. White pepper can be bought ready ground, but black pepper should always be ground freshly, as should nutmeg.

For making curries, unless you are really keen, it is easier (and cheaper) to buy jars of ready mixed spices in powder or paste form.

TO STORE

All spices should be stored in airtight jars, for no more than 6 months.

SPINACH

TO BUY

Fresh loose spinach should feel resilient and squeaky when pressed. Packs of spinach leaves are available, but check them carefully as any deterioration taints the whole pack. You will need about 150 g (6 oz) per person to cook, or 50 g (2 oz) per person for salads. For salads, choose small leaves. You can also buy frozen chopped spinach, which is quite tasty and useful for cooking.

TO STORE

Spinach can be stored for up to 24 hours in a fridge. Packs should be opened and transferred to a fresh bag or bowl. It can be frozen for 12 months, ideally after chopping.

TO PREPARE

Loose spinach should be washed in several changes of water, as it can be sandy. Fill a large bowl with cold water and swish the spinach round in it with your hands. For salads, nip the leaves from the stems and use whole. For cooking, tear the stems and central ribs from the leaves.

TO COOK

Put the leaves into a large saucepan with no more water than is left on them after washing. Add salt and butter if desired, cover the pan tightly and cook over medium heat for 3 - 5 minutes, shaking the pan at intervals. Turn the cooked spinach out into a colander and press it with a wooden spoon to remove excess liquid before serving.

WILTED SPINACH AND RAISIN STARTER

25 g (1 oz) raisins
300 g (12 oz) fresh spinach
25 g (1 oz) butter

25 g (1 oz) pine nuts
black pepper

Put the raisins in a bowl and cover them with boiling water, then leave them for 30 minutes to plump up. Prepare the spinach as above and shake off as much water as you can. In a large frying pan or wok, melt the butter and fry the pine nuts over medium heat for a couple of minutes, until they start to colour. Drain the raisins and cover them again with boiling water to warm them through. Put the spinach in the frying pan and toss it with the pine nuts until all the leaves have wilted. Turn it out onto a serving dish or plates, and grind black pepper over it generously. Drain the raisins and sprinkle them over the spinach before serving. Serve straightaway.

STOCK

TO BUY

In the better class of supermarket you can buy fresh liquid stock. Otherwise all you can buy is stock cubes, which are a poor substitute for making your own. Commercial stock cubes are convenient, but often contain a high proportion of salt and artificial flavour 'enhancers'.

TO STORE

Home-made stock can be kept for several days in the fridge, or in the freezer for 2 weeks if highly seasoned, up to 3 months if not.

TO MAKE STOCK

The basic principle of making stock is to simmer the ingredients for a long time, resisting the temptation to stir, which can make the stock cloudy. Start by putting the ingredients in a saucepan with enough water to cover them, bring the water to the boil, then turn it down to simmer and put a lid on the pan. When the stock is cooked, strain it, throwing away the solid bits. Then simmer it, uncovered, to reduce it and concentrate the flavour. Don't add salt when making stock.

FISH STOCKS
Fish stocks are usually made from trimmings, which can include heads and tails. For each 450 g (1 lb) fish trimmings, you need 750 ml (25 fl oz) liquid, (which can be all water or four parts water and one part white

wine), 1 onion, roughly chopped, 2 sticks of celery, roughly chopped, a few sprigs of parsley and a bay leaf.

MEAT OR CHICKEN STOCKS

Meat stocks are made from bones or scraps of meat. The bones can be raw or cooked, either bought specifically for stock-making or using the leftovers from a roast meal, such as a chicken. When using raw bones, they should be put in the pan with cold water and brought slowly to the boil. This will create a certain amount of scum, which should be skimmed off.

For each 450 g (1 lb) of bones, you need 750 ml (25 fl oz) water, 1 onion, 1 large carrot, and 1 stick of celery, all roughly chopped.

Meat stocks will inevitably contain some fat. The best way to remove this is to strain the liquid from the bones, then leave it to cool completely before putting it in the fridge overnight. The fat will rise to the top and solidify and can be removed easily.

Some people like to add spices such as peppercorns and mace, or a bouquet garni to their stocks.

VEGETABLE STOCKS

The simplest vegetable stock is the water in which vegetables have been cooked. Another way to get good, virtually free, vegetable stock is to scrub your vegetables thoroughly before peeling them, then use the peelings to make stock. For each 450 g (1 lb) of vegetable pieces, you need 750 ml (25 fl oz) water. Chop all the ingredients before cooking them, especially if using outer stalks of celery or fennel.

Pumpkin or squash peelings make a good stock, as do carrots, celery, and fennel. Onions are good, but the skins will colour the stock orangey-brown. Potatoes tend to thicken stock, and their starch will settle when the stock is left to stand. Unless you intend to use it straightaway, it is not a good idea to make stock with cabbage, turnips or other members of the cabbage family, as it develops an unpleasant smell when left to stand.

STRAWBERRIES

TO BUY

Fresh strawberries should feel firm when gently touched, and there should be very little, if any, juice in the bottom of the punnet. They should smell sweet and fruity.

TO CLEAN

Strawberries should be rinsed just before use. If there are holes in the bottom of the punnet, rinse the whole punnet under a gently running cold tap, shake off the worst of the water and tip the berries onto double thickness kitchen paper. Roll them on the paper to dry them off. Unless you want to retain the leafy 'hull' for decorative purposes, nip this off with finger and thumb. Large berries can be sliced or quartered.

TO STORE

Fresh strawberries should not be stored for more than 24 hours, since they start to deteriorate as soon as they are picked. Strawberries can be frozen for up to 12 months, either individually or in boxes, but can only be used for cooking or purée after defrosting, since freezing makes the tissues collapse.

STUFFING

TO BUY

You can buy dried stuffing mixes based on bread and herbs, to which you only need add water and egg. Although adequate, they are not as good as making your own. Better supermarkets offer fresh ready-to-use stuffings at Christmas.

TO STORE

Packets of stuffing mix should be stored in a dry cupboard. Once opened, they should be carefully resealed, or the contents should be transferred to a sealed plastic bag, as they will absorb moisture from the atmosphere and become stale. Once made up, stuffing should be used straightaway.

TO PREPARE

To make your own bread-based stuffings, it is best to use fresh breadcrumbs rather than dried or toasted crumbs. Herbs can be fresh or dried. Stuffing which includes pork sausagemeat is sometimes called forcemeat. Other variations on stuffing include chestnuts (with turkey), sage and onion (with pork), chopped apple (with goose).

For forcemeat, you need 250 g (10 oz) sausagemeat, 50 g (2 oz) breadcrumbs, salt and pepper, and water or beaten egg to bind the stuffing.

For sage and onion stuffing, you need 100 g (4 oz) breadcrumbs, 1 large onion, finely chopped, 1 tablespoon dried sage, salt and pepper and water to bind.

For chestnut stuffing, you need 450 g (1 lb) cooked chestnuts, 450 g (1 lb) pork sausagemeat, 100 g (4 oz) breadcrumbs, salt and pepper and 1 beaten egg to bind the stuffing. You can add 1 finely chopped onion and/or 450 g (1 lb) apple.

TO COOK

Add the weight of the stuffing to the weight of the meat, and cook it as though it was all meat. (See relevant pages for meat cooking times.) Any extra stuffing can be formed into balls the size of a golfball, and placed round the meat to roast, or cooked in a separate tin.

It is wise not to fill large birds such as turkeys with stuffing, as the stuffing may prevent the interior of the bird cooking properly. This gives the risk of salmonella poisoning. With large birds, stuff only the neck cavity, and cook any spare stuffing separately.

SUGAR, SYRUPS AND HONEY

TO BUY

For most purposes, the only sugar you need in your store cupboard is granulated white. If you have a liquidiser or food processor, you can soon convert this into the finer crystals of caster sugar. Caster sugar is specified in many recipes because its finer texture incorporates itself more quickly into the other ingredients. Icing sugar is still the same stuff as white sugar, but has been ground even finer than caster sugar.

Brown sugar is not, as many health buffs would have you believe, any better for you than white sugar. The brown colouring comes from molasses (one of the early stages in cane sugar production), so brown sugar either comes from an early stage in the refining process, or is a mixture of white beet sugar and molasses. The darker brown it is, the more molasses it contains, and the moister and stronger tasting it will be. Some cake recipes call for soft brown sugar, or the darker and stronger tasting muscovado. Brown sugar can sometimes set into hard lumps – break these up in a liquidizer, or by putting them into a plastic bag and bashing it with a rolling pin or heavy saucepan.

Golden syrup is a thick liquid made from refined sugar. You can buy it as 'pouring syrup' which is a thinner texture and comes in squeezy bottles, or in tins (the cheapest). To measure amounts of syrup, stand the tin in the scales, note the weight, then do some arithmetic to arrive at the amount that should be left when you've removed what you need, and spoon out as much as you need. Using a warm spoon will make the syrup slip off the spoon quicker. Molasses is the syrupy stuff left over after the refining process. It comes in various shades of brown and strength of taste, from 'sweet light' to the thick, dark and slightly bitter 'blackstrap'. Golden syrup and molasses may be called treacle.

Honey comes in two densities – runny or thick. Buy whichever you prefer. There are various flavours available, depending on the type of flower the bees worked on. Acacia or orange blossom are the lightest flavours, and should only be used for spreading on bread and butter. Clover, heather or lavender are a little stronger and can be poured over Greek yoghurt for a simple dessert, and mixtures (which will probably just be labelled 'honey' or 'product of several countries') can be used to spread or as a sugar or syrup substitute in cooking.

Maple syrup has a tangy flavour of its own. For this reason, and because it is quite expensive, it should not be used as a sugar or syrup substitute in cooking, but kept for pouring over pancakes or waffles. Make sure that you are buying the real thing, not something labelled 'maple flavour syrup'.

TO STORE

If kept in an airtight container, sugars, syrups and honey will keep indefinitely. Syrup, runny honey and maple syrup will sometimes turn into crystals, but can be re-liquified by standing the container in a bowl of warm water.

SWEDE AND TURNIP

TO BUY

Although closely related, swedes and turnips are not interchangeable. Swedes are a purply brown outside, have yellow flesh inside, and taste quite sweet, whereas turnips are mostly white outside (they can have purplish bottom halves), have white flesh and a distinctly hot flavour. The older they are, the hotter they get, so turnips are best when young and small. It is not true that swedes lack taste until they 'have had a frost on them', and they taste the same no matter how big they are. Both should be firm and have no blemishes on their skins, and they should have had the merest trimming of tops and roots. The removal of great slices from top and bottom is usually done by greengrocers trying to sell off the last of a deteriorating batch!

TO STORE

Swedes and turnips can be stored for several days indoors, but after that they tend to dry out and wrinkle. If you have somewhere dry outside where you can store them, they will keep for 4 - 6 weeks.

TO CLEAN AND PREPARE

Scrub off any dirt under cold water, then top and tail each root before peeling it. Swedes are most easily dealt with by using a heavy knife to cut them into manageable portions before peeling. The older and larger the root, the tougher the skin will be and the more you will have to remove. Drop each piece into water after peeling to prevent it drying out.

TO COOK

Small turnips should be boiled whole for 15 - 20 minutes, then drained and returned to the saucepan with a knob of butter (and, if you like, a tablespoonful of brown sugar) to glaze them before serving. Larger turnips, and swedes, should be cut into manageable chunks before boiling. They can be served with butter as above, or mashed on their own or with potatoes or carrots. They can also be added to stews.

SWEETCORN

TO BUY

Sweetcorn is the name for the individual kernels from corn on the cob. In America, where corn is inexpensive, people buy cobs and scrape the kernels off themselves. In this country, unless you grow your own or live close to a 'pick-your-own' farm, that tends to be a rather expensive way of getting something that is inexpensive to buy frozen or in tins.

TO COOK

Tinned or frozen sweetcorn can be served as a vegetable on its own, or mixed with peas. It can also be used for corn fritters. Fresh sweetcorn can also be used for these purposes, or to make corn pudding.

CORN FRITTERS

50 g (2 oz) plain flour
2 tablespoons milk
1 egg yolk

salt and pepper
150 g (6 oz) sweetcorn
oil for frying

With the flour, milk and egg yolk, make a thick batter. Season it and stir in the corn. Heat a little oil in a frying pan and drop in tablespoonsful of the batter. Flatten this out to make a little cake and fry 2 - 3 minutes each side, until the fritters are golden brown. Drain on kitchen paper before serving with bacon or fried chicken.

See also Corn on the cob (page 61).

TOMATOES

TO BUY

For salads, buy any type of tomato except the elongated type called 'plum' tomatoes. They range from the enormous 'beefsteak' or 'marmande' to tiny 'cherries'. You can sometimes find small yellow salad tomatoes, although these may have rather tough skins. All of them should have shiny skins and look and feel plump.

For cooking, the type you buy should suit the job you want it to do. Beefsteak are good for frying, grilling or stuffing, as are any of the smaller varieties. Medium sized cherries are good for threading on skewers to grill or barbecue. To make purées or tomato sauce, the best type (if you can find them) are plum tomatoes.

You can also buy plum tomatoes in tins, either whole or chopped, or in cardboard cartons or glass jars as various thicknesses of sauce, purée or passata (sieved purée). Any of these are good store-cupboard stand-bys, and generally easier to use for soups and stews than fresh tomatoes.

Sun-dried tomatoes are useful for flavouring home-made breads, but are rather expensive.

TO STORE

Fresh tomatoes can be kept in the fridge for 5 - 7 days, or at room temperature for 3 - 4 days. Tomatoes for cooking can be kept, whole or puréed, in the freezer for up to 3 months.

TO PREPARE

Small and medium sized tomatoes are normally served in salads with their skins on, either whole or halved. Beefsteak tomatoes are served in salads sliced, and some people like to remove the skins with a very sharp vegetable peeler. The same applies to slices in sandwiches.

For frying or grilling, the skins can be left on.

For stews, soups and sauces, it is advisable to remove the skins before cooking. If you have a freezer, the easiest method of removing the skins is to freeze the tomatoes for at least 24 hours, until they are frozen right through. Then fill a bowl with hot water, drop each tomato in and count slowly to 5 before removing it. Nick it with a fingernail and the skin will slip off. Alternatively, drop each tomato first into a saucepan of boiling water for a count of 5, then into a bowl of very cold water. Nick the skin as above and the tomato will come out. To remove the pips, cut each tomato in half, then put a sieve over a bowl and squeeze the pips out into the sieve, adding the liquid that collects in the bowl to the cooking liquid.

TO COOK

Tomatoes can be grilled or fried, in either case first cut in half, or roasted in halves or whole. In stews, they can be cut into pieces if desired. For soups, they will cook more quickly in small pieces, and then need to be liquidized or sieved.

TURKEY

TO BUY

Fresh whole turkeys for roasting should have plump legs and breasts. Calculate the size of bird (frozen or fresh) to buy at a rate of 450 g (1 lb) per person. Choose an 'oven-ready' bird if possible. Otherwise, ask the butcher to remove the head and feet. You can also buy breast joints on the bone for roasting, or breast 'steaks' for grilling or frying, in which case you will need 150 - 225 g (6 - 8 oz) per person.

TO CLEAN

With whole birds, always look inside the cavity – there may be a packet of giblets in there. If so, remove it before rinsing the bird under cold running water. Joints or steaks should also be rinsed under cold water before cooking.

TO STORE

See chicken (page 58).

TO PREPARE

See chicken (Page 58). Frozen birds must be completely defrosted before cooking to avoid the risk of salmonella. This should be done at room temperature, and will take a minimum of 36 hours for a bird weighing 4 kilos (9 lbs). For larger birds, add 12 hours to this time for each additional 2 kilos (4 lbs).

TO STUFF

It is inadvisable to stuff the whole bird, as this can make it difficult to judge the cooking time, and either the stuffing or parts of the bird may not cook properly. So stuff only the breast, by opening out the fold of skin at the neck end and pushing the stuffing in against the breast. Use your hands to mould the stuffing into a rounded shape, then fold the neck skin back over it and underneath the bird, securing it with a skewer. (See also page 147, stuffings).

TO COOK

To roast a whole turkey, preheat the oven to 180°C/350°F/ Gas Mark 4. Place the bird on a rack in a roasting tin, and roast it until the juice runs clear when the thigh is pierced with a skewer. Baste it with the fat from the tin at intervals during cooking. A 4 kg (9 lb) bird will take 3 - 3 ½ hours to cook, a 6 - 8 kg (13 - 17 lb) bird will take 4 - 5 hours.

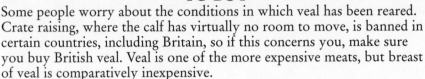

VEAL

TO BUY

Some people worry about the conditions in which veal has been reared. Crate raising, where the calf has virtually no room to move, is banned in certain countries, including Britain, so if this concerns you, make sure you buy British veal. Veal is one of the more expensive meats, but breast of veal is comparatively inexpensive.

British veal should be fine-textured, with deep pink flesh, and any fat should be white.

TO STORE

Veal can be kept in the fridge for up to 48 hours, or in the freezer for up to 12 months if in large pieces or 3 months if cubed or minced.

TO PREPARE

Because veal tends to have very little fat and has a delicate flavour that would be destroyed if it dries out during cooking, most of the preparation involves protecting it from drying out. With joints for roasting, the meat can be cooked with a layer of fat laid over it, or barded (strips of fat inserted into it with a needle). Smaller pieces of meat such as escalopes which are fried can be coated in breadcrumbs, or the meat can be slit open and stuffed. Escalopes are also frequently flattened by pounding them with a meat mallet (or heavy saucepan) before cooking so that they can be fried quickly.

TO COOK

Because of its tendency to dry out, veal is better pot-roasted or braised than roasted. A 1 kilo (2 lb) piece of veal will take 60 - 90 minutes to braise in a medium hot oven. Larger pieces need another 20 minutes per half kilo (1 lb).

To fry veal escalopes, first flatten or crumb them as above, then heat 25 g (1 oz) unsalted butter for each scallop before adding the veal. Cook for 2 - 4 minutes each side before draining on kitchen paper and serving with a wedge of lemon.

OSSO BUCCO (serves 4)

This is a classic Italian dish, of stewed veal shin in a wine and tomato sauce.

2 tablespoons olive oil
2 - 3 cloves garlic, sliced
4 pieces of veal shin, 5cm (2")
   thick, cut straight across and
   including the marrow bone,
   or the equivalent in
   cubes of meat
1 stick celery and
   2 carrots, chopped

450 g (1 lb) tomatoes,
   peeled and chopped
300 ml (10 fl oz) dry white wine
small bunch fresh herbs
   (thyme, marjoram, parsley)
salt and black pepper
2 teaspoons sugar (optional)
2 tablespoons chopped
   parsley for serving

In a large saucepan, heat the oil and fry the garlic for about 1 minute, then lay the meat in the pan and brown it on both sides. Add the celery, carrot and tomato and stew for 5 minutes until the tomatoes are breaking down into a sauce. Pour in the wine, add the bunch of herbs, bring the whole thing to the boil and season, adding some sugar if you feel the need. Then turn down the heat to a gentle simmer, cover the pan and cook for 2 ½ to 3 hours, until the meat is tender.

To serve, use a slotted spoon to lift out the pieces of meat onto hot plates before spooning out the sauce and sprinkling the parsley on top. Serve with mashed potato, noodles or rice.

VINAIGRETTE

AND OTHER SIMPLE SALAD DRESSINGS

Vinaigrette is, quite simply, a mixture of olive oil and wine vinegar, seasoned with salt and freshly ground black pepper. The classic proportion is 4 parts of oil to 1 part of vinegar. However, you can vary this, or the oil or vinegar you use, according to your taste, and you can add various other ingredients, again according to your taste.

You can use up to 6 parts oil to 1 part of vinegar, and change all or some of the oil to grape seed, walnut or hazelnut oil, or sesame seed oil for an oriental salad.

You can substitute lemon juice for vinegar, or use red wine, sherry, or cider vinegar or balsamic vinegar.

You can substitute soy sauce for salt, and white pepper for black pepper.

You can add mustard powder, crushed garlic, chopped herbs, or finely chopped chilli peppers – or any other flavouring that takes your fancy!

Whatever you use to make your vinaigrette, the oil and vinegar will separate whilst standing, so put all the ingredients into a screw top jar, put the lid on firmly, give the jar a good shake straightaway, then another good shake just before adding the dressing to the salad.

These salad dressings will keep for several days in the fridge.

VINEGAR

TO BUY

The most easily found vinegars are malt vinegar (from beer), and wine vinegar (red or white), but you can also buy cider vinegar, sherry vinegar, rice wine vinegar and balsamic vinegar. Real vinegar is a by-product of the drinks industry, and it is actually a dilute form of acetic acid. Some products which contain vinegar actually say 'acetic acid' or 'non-brewed condiment' rather than 'vinegar' in the list of contents, and this can be an indication that the taste will be harsh.

Malt vinegar is mainly used for pickling, or as a condiment. Wine vinegar is used for salad dressings and cooking. Cider vinegar is called for in some vegetarian recipes. Sherry and rice wine vinegar can usually only be found in specialist delicatessens. Balsamic vinegar can now be found in most supermarkets. It is made by the simple process of evaporation through the wood of the barrels in which it is stored – the longer the process takes, the better the flavour, and also the higher the cost! However, a good balsamic vinegar is so smooth and soft that you could almost drink it. It is mainly used in salad dressings.

You can also buy flavoured vinegars such as tarragon vinegar, raspberry vinegar or chilli vinegar, with or without the flavouring agent still in the bottle, or you can make these up yourself. Simply put a small bunch of herbs, a few chilli peppers or a few raspberries in a glass jar, fill it with white wine vinegar, seal it and leave it to stand for a couple of weeks before straining it and throwing away the herbs or fruit (these should not be left in, as they may hold tiny bubbles of air which carry botulism). Use it sparingly in salad dressings.

YOGHURT

TO BUY

Yoghurt is a good low-calorie substitute for cream, but only in its natural state. Flavoured yoghurts can contain a large amount of sugar, so if calorie control is desirable, check the contents list on the pots. Commercial yoghurt is often made with skimmed and powdered milk and thus lacks the creaminess of yoghurt made from whole milk. Greek yoghurt tends to be the creamiest. If you are fond of fruit yoghurts, it is cheaper to buy plain yoghurt and fruit compotes or low calorie jams and mix your own.

TO STORE

Yoghurt should be kept in the fridge. Unopened foil-sealed pots will keep for many weeks, but once opened it should be eaten within 48 hours.

TO MAKE YOUR OWN YOGHURT

Although you can buy special electric yoghurt makers, all you really need in the way of equipment to make your own yoghurt is a cooking thermometer, a wide necked vacuum flask and the patience to watch the milk simmer for 30 minutes or a 'milk saver' to prevent it boiling over. You need 600 ml (1 pt) of milk and 1 tablespoon of live natural yoghurt as a starter (or a tablespoon of home-made yoghurt).

Put the milk in a large saucepan (with the milk saver if you have one) and bring it to the boil, then turn it down to simmer for 30 minutes, or until it has reduced to two-thirds of its volume. Pour it out into a jug and stand this in a bowl of cold water. Put the thermometer in the jug and wait until the temperature has dropped to 44°C/115°F. Put the tablespoon of natural yoghurt in the vacuum flask, add 2 - 3 tablespoons of the cooled milk, stir well and add the rest of the milk. Put the lid on the flask and leave it for at least 6 hours, by which time you will have a flask full of yoghurt.

NB – If you use UHT (long-life) milk, you need only bring it to a temperature of 44°C/115°F and can omit the 30 minutes simmering.

TO COOK WITH YOGHURT

Yoghurt is a good sauce thickener and also features in many recipes for Indian food. However, it tends to separate if put into boiling liquid. Prevent this by first mixing 1 tablespoon plain flour into each 150 ml (5 fl oz) yoghurt.

TO MAKE CHEESE FROM YOGHURT

You can make your own soft cheese from natural live yoghurt (or from full-cream milk which has separated). All you have to do is put the yoghurt (or milk) in butter muslin or a purpose-made jelly bag and hang it up overnight to let the watery liquid drain off. Put a bowl underneath to catch the drips, but throw the liquid away. When the liquid has finished dripping out, turn the cheese into a dish and add salt and chopped herbs. Keep it in the fridge in a sealed pot.

INDEX